Presented to:

_____

Presented by:

_____

Date:

_____

D0009179

GOD'S ROAD MAP FOR LIFE

David Bordon and Tom Winters

WARNER
Faith®

New York Boston Nashville

God's Road Map for Life

Concept: David Bordon and Tom Winters

Project Writing: Deborah Webb and Rebecca Currington in association with SnapdragonGroup℠ Editorial Services

Warner Faith
Time Warner Book Group
1271 Avenue of the Americas, New York, NY 10020
Visit our Web site at www.warnerfaith.com

The Warner Faith name and logo are registered trademarks of the Time Warner Book Group.

Printed in the United States of America
First Warner Books printing: February 2006
10 9 8 7 6 5 4 3 2 1

ISBN:0-446-57888-6

LCCN: 2005934175

INTRODUCTION

The road of life, as you know if you've been walking on it for very long, has many unmarked intersections and cross streets. Not only that, but it weaves up, down, and around through all types of landscapes and terrains. The journey provides moments of breathtaking beauty and others of abject fear. There are dark stretches, detours and, of course, the danger of getting lost. What's a traveler to do? Happily, God has provided a road map—the Bible—to help us avoid dangerous and time-consuming delays and keep us on the path to our desired destination.

In *God's Road Map for Life*, we have mined the Bible for wisdom and understanding that will be helpful on your journey. We've included scriptures on certain topics you may have questions about and laid them out in an A-to-Z format so they will be simple for you to find and follow. We've also added to each topic an illustrative Bible story or practical devotional to help you on your way. Finally, we've provided heartfelt prayers and letters that express some of the thoughts and feelings God has expressed in His Word that we hope will inspire and encourage you.

We hope you will find all you need as you travel the road of life and reach your eternal destination safely. We'll be praying for you!

The Publishers

CONTENTS

Ambition

Aim for perfection, listen to my appeal, be of one mind, live in peace.
And the God of love and peace will be with you.

2 Corinthians 13:11

May God grant you your heart's desire,
and fulfill all your plans.

Psalm 20:4 NRSV

Make it your ambition to lead a quiet life, to mind your own business
and to work with your hands, just as we told you, so that your daily life
may win the respect of outsiders and so that you will not be
dependent on anybody.

1 Thessalonians 4:11-12

Don't lose a minute in building on what you've been given,
complementing your basic faith with good character,
spiritual understanding, alert discipline, passionate patience,
reverent wonder, warm friendliness, and generous love, each dimension
fitting into and developing the others.

2 Peter 1:5-7 THE MESSAGE

All hard work brings a profit.

Proverbs 14:23

Jesus said, "Do not work for food that spoils, but for food that endures
to eternal life, which the Son of Man will give you. On him God the
Father has placed his seal of approval."

John 6:27

ANOTHER DEFINITION

Ambition is a tricky concept—especially for those who earnestly desire to live for Jesus. Its primary definition suggests simply a strong yearning to achieve a particular end. In the Christian context, then, there is certainly nothing wrong with it. No doubt, every noble effort and every lofty deed begins with Christian ambition.

You might, for instance, make it your ambition to become the most understanding and encouraging supervisor on staff within your organization. As was the case with Joseph, you aspire to rise in rank by the sheer impact of your integrity and the inevitable outcome of a respectable work ethic. Your motive is inarguably pure, and your goals are completely considerate of others' success.

However, *ambition* has another definition that reveals itself in the Bible story of Joseph and his brothers. (See Genesis 37.) Jealous because Joseph was the favorite of their father, these young men sold their sibling as a slave to a traveling caravan on its way to Egypt. An ardent craving for rank, position, and power ended in an unthinkable act of betrayal.

One of the New Testament writers penned the following: "Make it your ambition to lead a quiet life, to mind your own business and to work with your hands" (1 Thessalonians 4:11). Isn't it fascinating that this ambition is propped up with scriptures addressing brotherly love on the one side and Christ's return on the other? Since the Lord is coming back, make it your ambition to live humbly . . . and love deeply.

Celebration

One generation will commend your works to another;
they will tell of your mighty acts.
They will celebrate your abundant goodness
and joyfully sing of your righteousness.

Psalm 145:4, 7

The father of the prodigal son said, "Let's have a feast and celebrate.
For this son of mine was dead and is alive again; he was lost
and is found." So they began to celebrate.

Luke 15:23-24

We praise you, LORD, for all your glorious power.
With music and singing we celebrate your mighty acts.

Psalm 21:13 NLT

The LORD, your God, is in your midst,
a warrior who gives victory;
he will rejoice over you with gladness,
he will renew you in his love;
he will exult over you with loud singing.

Zephaniah 3:17 NRSV

THE VICTORY IS OURS

Jesus commissioned seventy-two of His followers to go "ahead of him to every town" to heal the sick and announce that the King was coming. (See Luke 10:1.)

Something unexpected happened that resulted in a spirit of celebration among them. "The seventy-two returned with joy and said, 'Lord, even the demons submit to us in your name'" (Luke 10:17). Jesus hadn't commissioned them to exorcise demons. It was their faith in Him that, when put into action, had taken them deeper into the mission than they had thought to go. While they had been sent simply to tell those in captivity that the Deliverer was coming, they ended up on the front lines, doing battle with the enemy . . . putting his minions to flight!

The story doesn't end there. Jesus celebrated over them, as well. "Full of joy through the Holy Spirit," He praised the Father for their participation in the victory that would eventually overcome the world (Luke 10:21).

There is no joy as passionate as that of captives who have been set free. For hearts once held hostage in the miserable clutches of sin, selfishness, and Satan, the celebration of redemption is an exhilarating, expressive, and abundant jubilee of the Spirit. However, the experience of these disciples proves that there is one dimension of that joy which affords an even greater delight. It consists not only of one's own rescue, but also of participating by faith in overcoming the enemy on behalf of others who are still in captivity.

Celebration is never sweeter than when the victory is shared by all!

Challenges

Consider it a sheer gift, friends, when tests and challenges come at you from all sides. You know that under pressure, your faith-life is forced into the open and shows its true colors. So don't try to get out of anything prematurely. Let it do its work so you become mature and well-developed, not deficient in any way.

JAMES 1:2-4 THE MESSAGE

Jesus said, "I've told you all this so that trusting me, you will be unshakable and assured, deeply at peace. In this godless world you will continue to experience difficulties. But take heart! I've conquered the world."

JOHN 16:33 THE MESSAGE

You, dear children, are from God and have overcome them, because the one who is in you is greater than the one who is in the world.

1 JOHN 4:4

Despite all these things, overwhelming victory is ours through Christ, who loved us.

ROMANS 8:37 NLT

I can do everything with the help of Christ who gives me the strength I need.

PHILIPPIANS 4:13 NLT

Heavenly Father,

To me a challenge is a 10K run, not a car that runs out of gas in the middle of nowhere. It's learning a new language or preparing a new dish or playing an edgy game of softball, not sitting in the emergency room with a sick child or trying to make my salary extend to meet my bills. Sometimes challenges look a lot like problems. Just the same, I want to begin to think of them all—planned or unplanned, pleasant or unpleasant—as opportunities to respond in ways that are pleasing to You.

I ask You, Lord, to help me see the lesson in every challenge, the silver lining in every trial, the wonder of Your loving presence in every situation. Show me how to see my challenges as a way to become a better person.

Amen.

ALL SHAPES AND SIZES

Does it seem to you that life is fraught with challenges? Just about the time you think you've dealt with one, another pops up in its place. And challenges come in all shapes, sizes, and sorts.

With what do you answer those challenges?

Paul had a suggestion you might consider in Ephesians 3:16-19. Break it down so you can really digest it. (The actual scripture is in italics.)

- *Pray*—pour your heart out to the Lord
- *that out of his glorious riches*—His unlimited resources
- *he may strengthen you*—prepare you for action
- *with power*—supernatural vigor, energy, stamina, ability
- *through his Spirit*—His presence so near you can feel His breath on your face
- *in your inner being*—deep inside, where the impulse of your heart throbs in concert with the movement of His Spirit
- *so that Christ*—the crucified Jesus
- *may dwell in your hearts*—come fully alive in you
- *through faith*—a mysterious confidence that defies all logic
- *that you, being rooted and established in love*—the only justifiable motive
- *may have power*—supernatural vigor, energy, stamina, ability
- *to grasp*—take hold of with determination
- *how wide and long and high and deep*—every dimension
- *is the love of Christ*—the most powerful force in the universe
- *and to know this love*—experientially, profoundly, intimately
- *that surpasses knowledge*—reaches beyond reason or rationale
- *that you may be filled to the measure of all the fullness of God*—ready to face any challenge and overcome it!

My Precious Child,

Challenges are opportunities—opportunities to become strong and capable and confident. Without them, you would become weak and undisciplined. Your enemy would soon be walking all over you. And that's the point of challenges, really, to make sure you can stand up to and overcome whatever comes against you.

See your challenges as spiritual training, designed to strengthen your faith muscles. And while you're in the middle, don't look behind you or to the side. Instead, look up. I'm always waiting to help you. All you have to do is ask. I may not remove the challenge, but I will certainly help you make a championship showing.

Your loving Father

Change

Don't become so well-adjusted to your culture that you fit into it without even thinking. Instead, fix your attention on God. You'll be changed from the inside out. Readily recognize what he wants from you, and quickly respond to it. Unlike the culture around you, always dragging you down to its level of immaturity, God brings the best out of you, develops well-formed maturity in you.

Romans 12:2 THE MESSAGE

Jesus said, "I tell you the truth, unless you change and become like little children, you will never enter the kingdom of heaven. Therefore, whoever humbles himself like this child is the greatest in the kingdom of heaven."

Matthew 18:3-4

God . . . is looking for those with changed hearts and minds. Whoever has that kind of change in his life will get his praise from God.

Romans 2:29 TLB

Once you were less than nothing; now you are God's own. Once you knew very little of God's kindness; now your very lives have been changed by it.

1 Peter 2:10 TLB

THINGS HAD TO CHANGE

There is a lot of discussion about change these days. Within the span of one generation, Americans experience radical cultural, philosophical, and organizational shifts in just about every dimension of life—in family dynamics, churches, government, media, education, and business. What the experts want us to believe is that change is essential. "Change, or you risk becoming obsolete and unnecessary," they tell us.

However, change isn't new, nor is the need for it a novelty. God has been dealing with change from the very beginning. When Adam plunged the human race into sin in Eden, things had to change. When Noah was the only righteous man on the earth, things had to change. When Babel was built upon the pride of men's ego, things had to change. And on and on it goes.

Then one day, the kingdom of God appeared, and (you guessed it!) things had to change. John the Baptist said it in Matthew 3:2: "Repent (change your way of living), for the kingdom of heaven is near." The apostle Paul said it in Colossians 3:2: "Set your mind on things above, not on earthly things (change your way of thinking)." Jesus said it in John 4:23: "A time is coming and has now come when the true worshipers will worship the Father in spirit and in truth (change your perspective on God)."

If the words of Jesus are true for you—"the kingdom of God is within you"—then you must change too. So, change your way of thinking; think of others. Change your way of living; live for others. Change your perspective on God; there is no other.

Character

Be imitators of God [copy Him and follow His example],
as well-beloved children [imitate their father]. And walk in love,
[esteeming and delighting in one another] as Christ loved us and gave
Himself up for us, a slain offering and sacrifice to God.

Ephesians 5:1-2 AMP

Dear friend, do not imitate what is evil but what is good.
Anyone who does what is good is from God.

3 John 1:11

This is love for God: to obey his commands. And his commands are not
burdensome, for everyone born of God overcomes the world.

1 John 5:3-4

Jesus said, "'Love the Lord your God with all your heart, soul,
and mind.' This is the first and greatest commandment.
The second most important is similar: 'Love your neighbor as much as
you love yourself.' All the other commandments and all the demands
of the prophets stem from these two laws and are fulfilled if you obey
them. Keep only these and you will find that you
are obeying all the others."

Matthew 22:37-40 TLB

DON'T FORGET YOUR RAISIN'

"Do you want to grow up to be like your father . . . ?"

Did you ever hear a mother ask that? Of course. Then she elaborated on a list of behaviors which, if practiced consistently, would turn into habits and end up forging a dignified character.

"Keep your word, no matter what."

"Pay back ever' penny you owe."

"Work hard, harder'n all the rest."

"Never tell a lie, not even a little 'un."

"Don't cheat nobody."

"Don't forget your raisin'."

"Take your hat off when the flag passes by."

"Never look a gift horse in the mouth."

In much the same way, the Lord penned a list of behaviors for His people that, if practiced faithfully, would turn into habits of holiness and end up forging the godly character of a child of the Almighty. They are the ten sayings of Sinai:

I. Know no other gods; there aren't any.

II. Don't offer your worship to false gods; not your job, not your money, not your power, not yourself.

III. Respect the name of the Lord your God; it is a powerful source of blessing.

IV. Rest in the Lord your God, and learn to trust Him.

V. Treat your parents with love and respect, no matter what they've done.

VI. Don't murder or even show disrespect.

VII. Be faithful; keep your love at home.

VIII. Don't take what isn't yours; you didn't earn it.

IX. Don't slander others; be loyal.

X. Don't crave the things others have; be content.

Church

God gave me the work of telling all people about the plan for his secret, which has been hidden in him since the beginning of time. He is the One who created everything. His purpose was that through the church all the rulers and powers in the heavenly world will now know God's wisdom, which has so many forms. This agrees with the purpose God had since the beginning of time, and he carried out his plan through Christ Jesus our Lord.

Ephesians 3:9-11 NCV

Christ loved the church and gave himself up for her to make her holy, cleansing her by the washing with water through the word, and to present her to himself as a radiant church, without stain or wrinkle or any other blemish, but holy and blameless.

Ephesians 5:25-27

Christ is the head of the church, his body, of which he is the Savior. …We are members of his body.

Ephesians 5:23,30

All of you together are the one body of Christ, and each one of you is a separate and necessary part of it.

1 Corinthians 12:27 TLB

Heavenly Father,

I hear people talking about how important it is to go to church, but I don't see the point. After all, I can talk to You anytime I want and anywhere I want. I don't have to be in a fancy building with a lot of people around to feel Your presence or appreciate what You bring to my life. Is it really so bad if I just take a pass on the Sunday morning business? Honestly, Lord, I think I get more out of just enjoying some quiet time with You.

Still . . . I want to please You in everything I do. If there is something I'm missing by not being in church, please help me to see it. I promise to open my heart to hear what You want to say to me about this.

Amen.

BABEL'S LEGACY

It is just after the Flood, in the plain of Shinar. All the inhabitants of the earth speak the same language and live in the same region. They build "a tower whose top will reach into the heavens" in the name of mankind, that they may preserve their dominion on the earth (Genesis 11). The people unite to become a mighty power; however, theirs is a self-made sovereignty built on the arrogance of self-sufficiency. Those who should comprise the Church of the Almighty put their confidence in man, instead.

The heresy evokes a radical response from heaven. The Lord descends to disrupt their communication, causing all to speak in different tongues. Division erupts, the work is abandoned, and the people scatter, after all.

More than two thousand years pass. It is Pentecost, in Jerusalem, just after Jesus' resurrection. All the inhabitants of the earth speak different languages, and all are scattered abroad. God descends from heaven to reverse the heresy of Babel. The Spirit of the Lord is poured out upon men whose many tongues speak forth one message bringing all nations back together (Acts 2). The Lord erects a living edifice through which He reaches from heaven to earth and unites all believers in one name—Jesus. Empowering His people to be a mighty force for good, His sovereignty is reestablished upon the earth. The spiritual tower comprised of grateful souls is the Church of the redeemed.

God's plan to build a Church was established ages ago. God's plan to return for His Church is established in ages to come. Today, His Church is ours to enjoy—a haven for spiritual growth and community.

My Precious Child,

Meeting together with other believers is important—very important—but maybe not for the reasons you think. It's all about the power of two. All of your prayers have power, but when you pray with someone else or with a group of believers, the effectiveness of that prayer on the outcome is multiplied exponentially. The same is true with worship. When you worship Me alone, I hear you and take pleasure in your praise. But when you worship Me in unison with other believers, your praises create an environment of praise in which you are also blessed.

You need the perspective on the Christian life that comes from the pastor's sermon and the input of others. But most of all, you need a Christian family to support and encourage you. Don't shortchange yourself, My child. Choose church.

Your loving Father

Commitment

Every bit of my commitment is for the purpose of building you up,
after all, not tearing you down.
2 Corinthians 10:8 THE MESSAGE

What happens when we live God's way? He brings gifts into our lives,
much the same way that fruit appears in an orchard—things like affection
for others, exuberance about life, serenity. We develop a willingness to
stick with things, a sense of compassion in the heart, and a conviction
that a basic holiness permeates things and people. We find ourselves
involved in loyal commitments, not needing to force our way in life,
able to marshal and direct our energies wisely.
Galatians 5:22-23 THE MESSAGE

A friend is always loyal, and a brother is born to help in time of need.
Proverbs 17:17 NLT

Many will say they are loyal friends,
but who can find one who is really faithful?
Proverbs 20:6 NLT

If you love someone, you will be loyal to him no matter what the cost.
1 Corinthians 13:7 TLB

EMMA'S SENTRIES

She watched them through the window of the Neonatal Intensive Care Unit—two young men tying on surgical gowns. In their early twenties, they were obviously brothers—black hair, dark glistening eyes, and lean, muscular builds.

They had come every day for almost a month, ever since the arrival of the infant in Unit 2B. As a nurse, she had seen hundreds of people come and go; but these two intrigued her. They stood over the baby like sentries, as if guarding her from predators, kidnappers, or perhaps the angel of death. One after the other, they took turns reaching through the gloves in the incubator wall to stroke her tiny leg—no thicker than one of their fingers—or to touch her delicate cheek. Bending over her latex crib, they spoke to her in muffled tones, even singing softly, at times.

With every passing day, the infant grew weaker, her breathing became more labored, her chances for survival dimmer. Still the guardians appeared each afternoon, waiting for the 2:00 buzzer, whereupon they entered silently and walked resolutely to their post; never budging from their duty station until the hour had expired.

One Tuesday, she noticed one of the brothers wiping tears from his cheek. She quietly made her way to his side.

"Are you okay?" she inquired.

"Yeah," he looked away.

"I think it is awesome that you two come here every single day," she said. "Where'd you learn that kind of commitment?"

The young man stared at her for a moment. Finally he responded, "I don't know much about commitment, Ma'am. The point is, this is our niece, Emma—she's our brother's baby daughter."

When you're committed to someone, you're there when they need you.

Communication

The right word at the right time
is like a custom-made piece of jewelry.
Proverbs 25:11 THE MESSAGE

Putting away falsehood, let all of us speak the truth to our neighbors,
for we are members of one another.
Ephesians 4:25 NRSV

A gentle word defuses anger,
but a sharp tongue kindles a temper-fire.
Proverbs 15:1 THE MESSAGE

Let your conversation be always full of grace, seasoned with salt,
so that you may know how to answer everyone.
Colossians 4:6

Let no evil talk come out of your mouths, but only what is useful for
building up, as there is need, so that your words may give grace
to those who hear.
Ephesians 4:29 NRSV

Gracious speech is like clover honey—
good taste to the soul, quick energy for the body.
Proverbs 16:24 THE MESSAGE

The quiet words of the wise are more to be heeded
than the shouts of a ruler of fools.
Ecclesiastes 9:17

IT'S ALL ABOUT HEART

Experts say that in order to become proficient in the art of communication, you must learn to pay close attention to the signals you send with your body language, voice inflection, listening posture, and eye contact. In addition, your attempts will be greatly enhanced by your ability to restate the response of the other, while mirroring their intensity and emotions. Finally, your effectiveness in sharing thoughts and ideas is dependent upon being courteous, clear, concise, concrete, complete, and correct.

The thought of focusing on all that self-conscious detail could be a little overwhelming. It could even be so distracting that you end up missing the interpersonal connection altogether. You'll be relieved to hear that there is a simpler and more powerful formula for communication with a proven track record:

"Therefore, as God's chosen people, holy and dearly loved, clothe yourselves with compassion, kindness, humility, gentleness and patience. Bear with each other and forgive whatever grievances you may have against one another. . . . And over all these virtues put on love, which binds them all together in perfect unity" (Colossians 3:12-14).

The shorthand version is: "Communicate with heart."

Pretty simple, wouldn't you say?

The fact is, if the intent of your heart is truly compassionate, always kind, genuinely humble, persistently gentle, extremely patient, thoroughly forbearing, lavishly forgiving, and unconditionally loving, it won't matter who it is, what it's about, when it happens, or where you are; your communication will be profoundly effective. It's all about heart.

Compassion

The LORD is good to everyone.
He showers compassion on all his creation.

Psalm 145:9 NLT

When Jesus went out He saw a great multitude; and He was moved with
compassion for them, and healed their sick.

Matthew 14:14 NKJV

This I recall to my mind,
Therefore I have hope.
Through the LORD's mercies we are not consumed,
Because His compassions fail not.
They are new every morning;
Great is Your faithfulness.

Lamentations 3:21-23 NKJV

Praise be to the God and Father of our Lord Jesus Christ,
the Father of compassion and the God of all comfort, who comforts us
in all our troubles, so that we can comfort those in any trouble with the
comfort we ourselves have received from God.

2 Corinthians 1:3-4

Heavenly Father,

I come to You today a broken person. My body is wracked with pain, and I feel that I'm being crushed under the weight of my circumstances. All I can do is kneel at Your feet and ask for Your compassion and mercy. Nothing else I've tried has helped—and I feel certain that You are the only One who can help me now.

Lift me up, Lord. Heal my body and my mind. Look down on Your child with a heart of pity and restore my hope in the beauty of life and Your goodness and generosity. I want to live again, feel again, be productive again. I place myself in Your capable hands, Lord. And I wait for Your kindness and compassion to be poured out on me.

Amen.

THE HOLY HAND OF GOD

At synagogue, a woman is present who has been bent for eighteen years with a spirit of infirmity. Hers is not a demonic spirit, but a weakened moral condition, which eventually led to this twisted psychological and physical condition. Had she possessed the inner strength with which to resist her sickly state of mind, her bondage could have been avoided. But having yielded to the weakness within, she became deformed in both spirit and body.

She is partitioned off in the outer perimeters of the building with the rest of the women, and because she is bent from her illness, she can't see the Teacher at all.

Fortunately for her, He is no ordinary Rabbi. Jesus' intuitive eye misses nothing. He spies the sickly woman in the farthest corner of the room and summons her forward.

With a voice of tender compassion, Jesus speaks words of healing and release. She hears, but stands still stooped, not certain what is expected. Suddenly, she feels upon her crooked spine the warmth of human flesh as His strong hand runs firmly down the center of her back. He stands her up straight. Suddenly she sees Him—eye to eye. In eighteen years she has not stood aright, but in the presence of the Almighty, her vision for God and her stature among society are restored.

There are those who might argue that pity moved the heart of Jesus to speak the words that released her from the spirit of infirmity, but there is no doubt, it was genuine compassion that moved Him to touch her twisted back with His holy hand.

My Precious Child,

I know you feel lost and alone, deep within a fog of suffering and disappointment. But you are not lost—and you have never been alone. I've been close by, watching you try to deal with the blows life has handed you and waiting for you to invite Me to help. I've seen every wound. I've heard all your cries of pain. And My heart has ached to reach out to you with love and compassion.

Things will begin to get better now—I promise you that. Some of your griefs will simply disappear, and others will be worked out over time. But we will walk the path of healing together. Continue to lean on Me, for I will not fail you.

Your loving Father

Confidence

Do not be afraid of sudden terror,
Nor of trouble from the wicked when it comes;
For the LORD will be your confidence,
And will keep your foot from being caught.
Proverbs 3:25-26 NKJV

In the fear of the LORD is strong confidence:
and his children shall have a place of refuge.
Proverbs 14:26 KJV

If God is for us, who can be against us?
Romans 8:31

Even though I walk through the darkest valley,
I fear no evil;
for you are with me;
your rod and your staff—
they comfort me.
You prepare a table before me
in the presence of my enemies.
Psalm 23:4-5 NRSV

SUPER-SIZED SIBLING

The younger of two brothers—a third grader—bolts into the house, slamming the door behind him. Panting wildly, he drops his books on the landing.

"What's up, Bud?" the older brother—a high-school junior—passes him on the stairs.

"This kid is after me," the little guy explains, bent over at the waist still catching his breath.

"Why? What'd you do?"

"I told him to stop beating on that brown cat from down the street. He says he's gonna smash my face in," the boy swipes his forehead; his face is blotched with fear.

"Where is he now?" the elder's protective ire is beginning to stir.

"Right behind me," he nods.

"Why don't you let me answer the door," says the older.

Simultaneously, the bell rings and a fist pounds the door.

The little bully is shocked when instead of his equal, he is greeted by a large chest, expanding into broad, muscular shoulders, upon which sits the imposing countenance of an intimidating, super-sized sibling.

"Yeah?" the big guy raises one eyebrow.

"Kyle here?" the kid squirms.

"Why do you need to know?" his deep voice shakes the boy to the soles of his shoes.

"I got some business with him, that's why," he tries to sound tough.

"Actually," the older boy lowers his chin and looks out from under his brow, "I'm Kyle's brother. If you got business with him, then you got business with me."

The boy leaps off the porch and runs like the wind.

Need confidence with which to face the battle? You have an older brother—His name is Jesus.

Contentment

Godliness with contentment is great gain, for we brought nothing
into the world, and we can take nothing out of it; but if we have food
and clothing, we will be content with that.

1 Timothy 6:6-8

I have learned the secret of contentment in every situation,
whether it be a full stomach or hunger, plenty or want; for I can do
everything God asks me to with the help of Christ who gives me
the strength and power.

Philippians 4:12-13 TLB

Keep your lives free from the love of money and be content
with what you have, because God has said,
"Never will I leave you; never will I forsake you."

Hebrews 13:5

Don't push your way to the front; don't sweet-talk your way to the top.
Put yourself aside, and help others get ahead.

Philippians 2:3 THE MESSAGE

THE BEST CANDIDATE

Janet was the captain of the cheerleading squad while her identical twin sister, Maggie, couldn't even turn a decent cartwheel. Maggie was intelligent, studious, and good-natured, but her vivacious sister was the popular one—always commanding the limelight.

One week prior to the student council elections, Maggie and Janet stood before the entire student body to deliver their campaign speeches. Maggie's comments were focused on the betterment of student/faculty relations, greater participation in extracurricular scholastic events, and a diligent campaign to raise the bar of academic achievement campus wide. Janet's speech, on the other hand, bore a resemblance to a pre-game pep rally. Not much content, but a whole lot of noise.

On election day, Janet stood at the polling box deliberating over her vote. Convinced that every vote counted, she wrote her own name on her ballot. Suddenly, her conscience bit her hard; she remembered her father's frequent counsel: "Be content with who you are, and you'll be free to celebrate the truth about other people." Janet knew her sister would be a better representative. After all, Maggie's diligence was her greatest virtue. As Janet scratched out her own name and wrote, "Maggie," a peculiar sense of peace filled her heart.

When the voice came blaring through the P.A. system announcing that Maggie had won, Janet grabbed her and gave her a huge, delighted hug.

Maggie shook her head, "What are you so happy about? You lost."

"The candidate I voted for won the election!" Janet answered.

"You voted for me?" Maggie's eyes widened.

"Let's face it, Mag; I'm a cheerleader, not a student council leader. I'll leave the council concerns to you if you'll leave the cartwheels to me!"

Courage

Don't lose your courage or be afraid. Don't panic or be frightened,
because the LORD your God goes with you, to fight for you
against your enemies and to save you.

Deuteronomy 20:3-4 NCV

LORD, you are my shield,
my wonderful God who gives me courage.

Psalm 3:3 NCV

Do not lose the courage you had in the past, which has a great reward.
You must hold on, so you can do what God wants and receive
what he has promised.

Hebrews 10:35-36 NCV

Be strong and courageous. Do not be afraid or terrified because
of them, for the LORD your God goes with you; he will never
leave you nor forsake you.

Deuteronomy 31:6

Be strong in the Lord and in the power of His might.
Put on the whole armor of God, that you may be able to stand
against the wiles of the devil.

Ephesians 6:10-11 NKJV

Keep alert, stand firm in your faith, be courageous, be strong.

1 Corinthians 16:13 NRSV

Heavenly Father,

I have so many dreams and aspirations, so many responsibilities and opportunities, but it seems like my feet are stuck in the mud. I just can't find the courage to move forward and do the things I should. My children need more guidance and correction, but I'm afraid that they won't like me. My boss needs to hear my ideas and opinions, but I'm afraid he won't like what I have to say. My friends and family are probably getting tired of my reluctance to make a decision—I'm afraid I'll make the wrong one. And forget about telling others about my relationship with You—what if they reject me?

Lord, I must be the most cowardly person on earth. I seem to be afraid of anything that moves, including my own shadow. Show me how to find my courage and become the strong, decisive person You created me to be.

Amen.

THE COURAGE THAT COMES FROM FAITH

The scrawny shepherd boy shouted at the giant with the confidence of youth: "You come against me with sword and spear and javelin, but I come against you in the name of the LORD Almighty, . . . whom you have defied. This day the LORD will hand you over to me, and . . . the whole world will know that there is a God in Israel . . . for the battle is the LORD's" (1 Samuel 17:45-47).

Where was that fearless boy when it was written of him as a man that he was fleeing from King Saul and very much afraid? (1 Samuel 21:10-12).

Common courage is a come-and-go characteristic. It visits you in the naïveté of youth when you feel invincible. However, it tends to dissipate with the accumulation of position and wealth, perhaps because you have the good sense to recognize the gravity of the risk. It may resurface in circumstances fraught with desperation. But, then again, it may not.

Common courage is a vacillating quality that you may or may not be able to muster when needed.

However, the courage that comes through faith is different. It is the result of a genuine understanding of the love and providence of the Almighty. "If God is for us, who can be against us?" (Romans 8:31).

The shepherd boy had the courage of genuine faith while out in the wild, observing daily the wonder and provision of God's creation. Once he joined the political realm of human endeavor in palatial surroundings of creature comfort, it seems he experienced a lapse in his intimate interaction with the Creator.

True courage must be cultivated through intimacy with and dependence on the Almighty.

My Precious Child,

Standing out there on that limb all by yourself can be a terrifying experience. But that's where your problem begins—you haven't yet realized that you are not alone! I'm with you all the way, helping you make decisions, stick to your convictions, meet your responsibilities, and share your faith. Of course you aren't strong enough, wise enough, or convincing enough to take on everything all at once—but I am!

The next time you feel your courage failing, picture Me standing there next to you. It's not a game—I really am there, urging you on, backing you up, helping you think through decisions. When you mess up—and you will at times—I'll be there to help you pick up the pieces and start again.

Your loving Father

Daily Walk

We know that our old self was crucified with him so that the body of sin might be done away with, that we should no longer be slaves to sin.

Romans 6:6

Once you were under God's curse, doomed forever for your sins. You went along with the crowd and were just like all the others, full of sin, obeying Satan, the mighty prince of the power of the air, who is at work right now in the hearts of those who are against the Lord. But God is so rich in mercy; he loved us so much that even though we were spiritually dead and doomed by our sins, he gave us back our lives again when he raised Christ from the dead.

Ephesians 2:1-2, 4-5 TLB

You were taught, with regard to your former way of life, to put off your old self, which is being corrupted by its deceitful desires; to be made new in the attitude of your minds; and to put on the new self, created to be like God in true righteousness and holiness.

Ephesians 4:22-24

Walk in the Spirit, and you shall not fulfill the lust of the flesh.

Galatians 5:16 NKJV

WALKING DAILY IN THE KINGDOM OF LIGHT

The Resurrection and Ascension of Jesus triggered the outpouring of the Holy Spirit at Pentecost, ushering in the reign of God's kingdom. King Jesus, who laid down His life to redeem the lost, and the Almighty *Abba*, who raised Him up by the power of love, now dwell within the hearts, minds, and souls of men through the Spirit of self-sacrifice. True believers live in the Spirit, rejoice in the Spirit, pray in the Spirit, hope in the Spirit, sing in the Spirit, speak in the Spirit, and walk according to the Spirit—the Spirit of the crucified King.

There is another kingdom which is alive and well upon this earth. It is the dominion of the prince of darkness. His is the self-serving spirit of self-exaltation, self-consumption, self-promotion, self-preservation, self-absorption, self-actualization, self-conceit, self-aggrandizement, self-awareness, self-assertion, self-consciousness, self-confidence, self-devotion, self-indulgence, and self-seeking—all in the self-centered service of self-love. Those who live in the flesh are likewise selfish.

These two kingdoms are in constant conflict over the souls of men in this present age. But in the days to come, the King Eternal will put an end to the kingdom of this world.

Your daily walk demonstrates your allegiance—to one king or the other. Day by day, even moment by moment, you choose which kingdom reigns within your heart. If you choose Jesus, then *self* and all of its modifiers are brought into submission to the Spirit—the self-sacrificing Spirit of the crucified King. But if you choose Satan, then *self* and its minions make their ascent and demands.

Guard against the self-deception of selfish ambitions that lead to self-destruction. The only trace of *self* in the Spirit's context is self under control.

Decisions

Jesus said, "Father . . . not My will, but Yours, be done."

Luke 22:42 NKJV

I am the LORD your God,
who teaches you what is best for you,
who directs you in the way you should go.

Isaiah 48:17

People throw lots to make a decision,
but the answer comes from the LORD.

Proverbs 16:33 NCV

I will instruct you and teach you in the way you should go;
I will counsel you and watch over you.

Psalm 32:8

Without counsel, plans go awry,
But in the multitude of counselors they are established.

Proverbs 15:22 NKJV

LIVING DECISIVELY

Often the greatest difficulty in making decisions has to do with selection. You can narrow the field a bit by eliminating those that are intrinsically wrong. Yet even among good choices, there are so many. Here are some tips to help you along the way:

- Realize that you automatically eliminate something else by dedicating yourself and your resources to the decision you make.

- In any arena in which you apply decision-making skills, you will benefit from remaining open to the input of others who demonstrate objectivity in their perspective and authentic concern for you.

- Be aware that indecision is, in fact, a decision to do nothing. If you procrastinate in making your decision, you are not only putting off progress, but you are choosing to let circumstances or other people determine your course of action for you. That is living by default rather than by decision.

- Making good decisions requires discernment on the front end and diligence for the long haul. Do not make the mistake of many who have allowed the pressures of society, the media, colleagues, friends, or family to make their decisions for them. And most importantly, don't let anyone discourage you from following through.

- Once the decision is made, keep your focus; don't look back and second-guess yourself. Instead, put yourself wholeheartedly into your selection so that you will have no regrets.

Take charge of your life, take courage in your ability to live it well, and take everything to God in prayer.

Doubt

Faith comes from hearing the message,
and the message is heard through the word of Christ.
Romans 10:17

Lord, when doubts fill my mind, when my heart is in turmoil,
quiet me and give me renewed hope and cheer.
Psalm 94:19 TLB

He has given us both his promise and his oath, two things we can
completely count on, for it is impossible for God to tell a lie.
Now all those who flee to him to save them can take new courage when
they hear such assurances from God; now they can know without doubt
that he will give them the salvation he has promised them.
Hebrews 6:18 TLB

Be merciful to those who doubt.
Jude 1:22 TLB

Jesus said, "Anything is possible if a person believes." The father
instantly replied, "I do believe, but help me not to doubt!"
Mark 9:23-24 NLT

Heavenly Father,

I believe in You with all my heart, I truly do. It's just that sometimes little doubts creep in. I wonder about some of the things I've read in the Bible, like oceans parting down the middle, the sun standing still, blind men seeing, and lame men walking. I don't know what to think about a virgin having a baby or dead people coming back to life.

I know this much, Lord. Nothing is impossible for You. If You chose to heal a blind man or part the ocean so Your people could pass through, I know it would have been easy for You. After all, You created this natural world in the first place.

No, Father, the problem is with me; I know it is. Expand my mind and banish the doubts that come from my small thinking. Help me to move from doubt to the full assurance of faith.

Amen.

DOUBT—A SERVANT OF FAITH

As human beings, we are subject to doubts. We ask ourselves questions and mull things over in our minds, all the while trying to build a logical framework around our known world. God, who created our minds, is aware of this tendency, and He not only condones it, He encourages it.

The most famous doubter was Thomas, one of Jesus' disciples, often referred to as "Doubting Thomas." After Jesus was resurrected from the grave, He appeared one night to His disciples. Thomas was not present, and when the others tried to convince him that Jesus was alive, he was not convinced. After all, he'd seen Jesus crucified, His body placed in a borrowed tomb sealed by an enormous boulder. The tomb was guarded around the clock by Roman sentries. As much as Thomas wanted to believe, to join in the jubilation all around him, he just couldn't. "Unless I see the nail marks in his hands and put my finger where the nails were, and put my hand into his side, I will not believe it," he told them (John 20:25).

When Jesus appeared again a week later, Thomas was there. Jesus did not rebuke Thomas. Instead He invited him to resolve his doubts. "Put your finger here; see my hands. Reach out your hand and put it into my side. Stop doubting and believe," Jesus told Thomas (John 20:27). That simple gesture was enough. Thomas's questions were answered, his doubts allayed. Beyond all logic and physical laws, a miracle had taken place—his Lord was alive!

Don't harbor your doubts. Bring them out in the open; talk to God about them. He can handle them!

My Precious Child,

Doubts come from your mind; faith comes from your heart. That's a big distinction because your mind is part of your natural self that is growing in understanding. As you spend time with Me, your mind will learn to see things in a different way. The day will come when you realize that My power can and does, at times, supersede the laws of nature, and your doubts will vanish.

Until then, relax and stop beating yourself up about it. I created your mind and its ability to question, to reason. If you didn't have some doubts, I would wonder if it were working properly. Stay close to Me. Bring your questions to Me, and we'll look at each one together.

Your loving Father

Encouragement

Glory in his holy name;
Let all rejoice who seek the Lord.
Seek the Lord; yes, seek his strength
And seek his face untiringly.

1 Chronicles 16:10-11 TLB

All who seek the Lord shall find him and shall praise his name.
Their hearts shall rejoice with everlasting joy. The whole earth shall see it
and return to the Lord.

Psalm 22:26-27 TLB

Those who know your name put their trust in you,
for you, O LORD, have not forsaken those who seek you.

Psalm 9:10 NRSV

The LORD looks down from heaven on humankind
to see if there are any who are wise,
who seek after God.

Psalm 14:2 NRSV

SPUR ON AND INSPIRE

These are the words King David spoke to encourage his son Solomon upon his ascension to the throne:

"Acknowledge the God of your father, and serve him with wholehearted devotion and with a willing mind, for the LORD . . . understands every motive behind the thoughts. If you seek him, he will be found by you; but if you forsake him, he will reject you forever. Consider now, for the LORD has chosen you. . . . Be strong and do the work" (1 Chronicles 28:9-10).

Encouragement by contemporary definition means to stimulate, spur on, and inspire with upbeat, motivational input. But by ancient standards, it meant much more. Spiritual encouragement is comprised of a balanced perspective on life here and in the hereafter, expounding upon what happens if you heed the words that inspire, and what happens if you don't. Try breaking it into bite-sized bits of inspiration.

Acknowledge God by:

· Serving Him with your whole heart and an open mind.
· Being honest, because He knows more about you than you know about yourself.
· Seeking Him . . . He wants to be pursued.
· Taking it very personally that the Lord has called you.
· Fulfilling your calling with all of your ability and all of your might.

True encouragement isn't a pep rally full of hype and slick promises. It is a strong provocation to move into action on behalf of something much greater than yourself.

Eternal Life

Jesus said, "This is eternal life: that they may know you,
the only true God, and Jesus Christ, whom you have sent."

John 17:3

Jesus said, "Those who drink of the water that I will give them will
never be thirsty. The water that I will give will become in them a spring
of water gushing up to eternal life."

John 4:14 NRSV

Jesus said, "Very truly, I tell you, anyone who hears my word and
believes him who sent me has eternal life, and does not come under
judgment, but has passed from death to life."

John 5:24 NRSV

This is the testimony: God gave us eternal life, and this life is in his Son.
Whoever has the Son has life; whoever does not have the Son of God
does not have life.

1 John 5:11-12 NRSV

Jesus said, "I came so they can have real and eternal life,
more and better life than they ever dreamed of."

John 10:10 THE MESSAGE

ETERNITY NOW

Talk to a roomful of twenty-year-olds about eternal life, and you are likely to get a nod of assent, an agreeable smile, and a polite handshake or two. But speak to a ward of terminally ill patients in the local hospital, and you'll probably find some passionate "amens," some tears of relief, and several heartfelt hugs.

Though it may seem like it, eternal life is not a concept of relativity. What makes it appear so is that people are relatively unconcerned about it until they feel the desperate need to know that it will be there—like a safety net—ready to catch them when they fall into the unknown abyss of death. And it will, no doubt about it. What is missed, though, is the understanding that eternal life is more than an after-life issue. Contrarily, it is a present reality—the only source of abundant living—for those who know the Lord.

For those who don't know Him, the words sound trite—like foamy platitudes brimming from a religious crock. But for those who do, a wistful sigh escapes at the mere mention of His name. Intimacy with God involves an encounter with Jesus—eye-to-eye, face-to-face, heart-to-heart. Knowing Jesus is abundant living—abundant peace, joy, love, mercy, hope, healing, and life.

What is your concept of eternal life? Is it real life now, or some faraway passing thought? God wants to give you all that He has planned for you—including a life worth living here on earth. Invite Him in, and eternity starts today.

Expectations

The LORD says,
"Anyone who trusts in me will not be disappointed."
Isaiah 49:23 NCV

The Lord GOD says:
"I will put a stone in the ground in Jerusalem, a tested stone.
Everything will be built on this important and precious rock.
Anyone who trusts in it will never be disappointed."
Isaiah 28:16 NCV

I lift up my eyes to the hills—
where does my help come from?
My help comes from the LORD,
the Maker of heaven and earth.
Psalm 121:1-2

Look to him, and be radiant;
so your faces shall never be ashamed.
Psalm 34:5 RSV

Heavenly Father,

I'm filled with frustration and anger. Tears are always close to the surface, and I'm not sure how long I can go on this way. It seems like no one keeps their promises or works as hard as they should or does what they're supposed to. And the worst thing of all is that I don't measure up either—to my own expectations.

Why am I like this, Lord? Why do I always want and expect more than I can have, more than anyone— including me—can possibly give? I know the people in my life are good people. They try to make me happy. Am I hopeless, Lord? How can I stop judging? Stop expecting? Stop crashing into disappointment? Start living my life?

Amen.

MAKE ME HAPPY

"What in heaven's name is going on?" Pastor Mike was of the opinion that Michelle and Larry had one of the most solid marriages in his congregation. Now she was in his office, in crisis.

"Larry left for work this morning, just like any other day; but when he got to his office, he called home." She paused to blow her nose into a tissue. "He said he is too tired to go on."

"Tired of what, Michelle?"

"I don't know," she cried.

"Is there someone else?" He felt it necessary to ask since there frequently was, but he didn't suspect it in Larry's case.

"No . . . " she bawled. "I almost wish there were. Then I would stand a fighting chance."

"What is it, then? You must have some idea."

"He said there's no use in trying anymore."

"Trying what?"

"To make me happy," her voice lowered at this admission.

"Have you been unhappy?" Mike was baffled. Michelle always wore a happy face at church. Come to think of it, though, there had always been a mysteriously synthetic quality about her cheerfulness.

Her silence spoke volumes to the seasoned counselor.

At last she spoke, "The truth is, I am unhappy; always have been. I just expected more from my marriage than Larry is capable of giving, I guess."

"Has it ever crossed your mind that you expected more than you were willing to give?"

Expectations can be deadly—common desires, when unchecked, propagate unreasonable demands. Ask God to help you realign your expectations. It's not too late to be really happy.

My Precious Child,

Your unrealistic expectations of yourself and those around you stem from insecurity deep down inside your heart. Learning to be satisfied with who you are won't happen overnight, but you're far from hopeless. Together we can make our way past the judgments, around the disappointments, through the bogus expectations, and onto the path to joy and contentment.

Where do we begin? By starting to see yourself and others through My eyes—the eyes of love. When you look at yourself in the mirror and realize you haven't lost those pounds you expected to lose, say to yourself, "It's all right because God loves me just the way I am." As you come to grips with your expectations for yourself, your expectations for others will come into balance as well.

Your loving Father

Faith

What is faith? It is the confident assurance that what we hope for is going
to happen. It is the evidence of things we cannot yet see.

Hebrews 11:1 NLT

"Have faith in God," Jesus answered. "I tell you the truth, if anyone says
to this mountain, 'Go, throw yourself into the sea,' and does not doubt
in his heart but believes that what he says will happen, it will be done for
him. Therefore I tell you, whatever you ask for in prayer, believe that you
have received it, and it will be yours."

Mark 11:22-24

Is any one of you sick? He should call the elders of the church
to pray over him and anoint him with oil in the name of the Lord.
And the prayer offered in faith will make the sick person well;
the Lord will raise him up.

James 5:14-15

We live by faith, not by sight.

2 Corinthians 5:7

We must always give thanks to God for you, brothers and sisters,
as is right, because your faith is growing abundantly.

2 Thessalonians 1:3 NRSV

WILL YOU TRUST HIM?

There are only a handful of times recorded in the Bible that you find Jesus surprised by the depth of someone's belief; and peculiarly, those instances always involve someone whose religious orientation should have excluded them from the realm of radical faith.

Such was the case with a certain Gentile soldier residing in the city of Capernaum—the home base of Jesus' early ministry. Perhaps he had heard with his own ears the unique authority with which Jesus spoke, or had witnessed a healing miracle. Whatever the case, the centurion made a request of some Jewish friends that they seek the Lord's help on behalf of his servant who was suffering terribly and was about to die.

Jesus listened as the messengers recounted how much the soldier had done for their people; even building them a synagogue in which to worship. He was moved to respond on his behalf and started toward the centurion's dwelling.

Having heard that the Lord had troubled Himself to walk the distance, the soldier sent an entourage to stop Him, saying, "Sir, I am undeserving of Your presence within my house. You need not trouble Yourself to come. Just say the word, and my servant will be healed."

Jesus was astonished! Here was a man who had been reared without the knowledge of God suggesting that He could work such a miracle with merely His word.

You may or may not have been raised in a community of faith. All that matters is what your faith is saying to you today. Will you trust Him with the affairs of your life? Will you trust Him with your heart?

Faithfulness

A talebearer reveals secrets,
But he who is of a faithful spirit conceals a matter.
Proverbs 11:13 NKJV

How thankful I am to Christ Jesus our Lord for . . . giving me the
strength to be faithful to him.
1 Timothy 1:12 TLB

If we are faithful to the end, trusting God just as we did when we first
became Christians, we will share in all that belongs to Christ.
Hebrews 3:14 TLB

O Jehovah, Commander of the heavenly armies,
where is there any other Mighty One like you?
Faithfulness is your very character.
Psalm 89:8 TLB

If we are faithless,
He remains faithful.
2 Timothy 2:13 NKJV

Oh, love the LORD, all you His saints!
For the LORD preserves the faithful.
Psalm 31:23 NKJV

IN THE FACE OF UNFAITHFULNESS

A harmful trend has taken hold. It runs rampant through broken relationships, leaving behind a path of destruction and ruin.

Having been dubbed by experts as *exposure*, this tendency really borders on exploitation. It holds forth the philosophy that when a violation has occurred in a relationship, each party may try to outdo the other with smear tactics and malicious gossip, to scandalize reputations, destroy financial securities, wreak havoc in third-party relationships, and obliterate any hope for a future.

A wife tells every undignified detail of her husband's affair to exonerate herself of responsibility. A husband maligns his spouse in front of the children to justify his unfaithfulness. An adult exposes the shameful sins of her father in order to get the attention she craves. A mother broadcasts her son's struggle with drug addiction to a women's prayer group out of resentment.

The idea of "confessing your sins to one another" has somehow been twisted into "confessing one another's sins, in lieu of one's own."

The problem is, this pattern conflicts with the character of the Faithful One. Faithfulness isn't reserved only for those who have been loyal to you. Faithfulness must be understood in the context of a God who is faithful in spite of extreme disloyalty.

"Mary was pledged to be married to Joseph, but before they came together, she was found to be with child through the Holy Spirit. Because Joseph her husband was a righteous man and did not want to expose her to public disgrace, he had in mind to divorce her quietly" (Matthew 1:18-19).

Faithfulness shines brightest in the face of unfaithfulness.

Fear

Don't be afraid, for I am with you. Do not be dismayed,
for I am your God. I will strengthen you. I will help you.
I will uphold you with my victorious right hand.

Isaiah 41:10 NLT

When I am afraid, I will put my confidence in you.
Yes, I will trust the promises of God.

Psalm 56:3-4 TLB

I call to you from the ends of the earth
when I am afraid.
Carry me away to a high mountain.
You have been my protection,
like a strong tower against my enemies.

Psalm 61:2-3 NCV

I am the LORD, your God,
who takes hold of your right hand
and says to you, Do not fear;
I will help you.

Isaiah 41:13

Heavenly Father,

I struggle so with fear and anxiety. Are my children safe? Is my spouse being faithful? Is the spot on my arm skin cancer? Will we be able to pay the bills? The list literally has no ending—it goes on and on and on. A friend said to me that we can't escape the dangers in this world, but we can place our trust in You. Faith trumps fear—that's what she said.

Lord, I want to divest myself of all these fears and anxieties I've been carrying around before I waste my life fretting over what might happen. I know this isn't going to be an overnight fix, but I've got to start somewhere. Each time a fearful or anxious thought enters my mind, I'm going to stop right there and offer it up to You. Nudge me, please, when I fail to do that. I want to be faithful, not fearful!

Amen.

THE BOTTOM OF THE STAIRS

The little girl ran up the stairs from where she sat in the basement, wheezing from fright. She wished desperately that her father hadn't put the piano down there where she despised to go. Her passion for music had once been so strong—so compelling—until the object of her devotion was submerged beneath the surface of the earth, into the damp, subterranean level of their home. Had she simply confided the fear, her father would have remedied it.

As a beginner, she would wait for another family member going into the basement for some lengthy errand: Mama tending to the wash, Dad tinkering in his workshop, her brothers engaged in a ping-pong duel. She practiced happily and skillfully as long as she had accompaniment. However, she always got lost in her music and failed to notice when her companions had finished their tasks and ascended back into the light of day. Suddenly, her intuition would stir, halting her fingers upon the keys, and always a moment too late. Paralyzed by the eerie silence for an instant, she would then bolt to her feet and run frantically up the flight of stairs.

After several months of fleeing the predator, her passion gave way. Fear had dogged her every step of progress, haunted her every moment of ecstasy, and finally quenched the fire within her. In desperation, she confided the fear to her father.

By the next afternoon, the piano had been moved to a sunny, comfortable space on the first floor. She wondered why she hadn't confessed her fears much sooner.

If you will simply confide the fear, your Father will help you escape it.

My Precious Child,

You're right about the world you live in—it's a dangerous place. The path is strewn with physical, mental, emotional, and spiritual perils. The potential for disaster is never more than a breath away. If you were on your own, you would have reason to be very afraid. But you aren't alone! I'm right here by your side.

My presence in your life brings with it the virtues of the kingdom. Instead of confusion, there is peace. Instead of hatred, there is love. Instead of evil, there is good. When you give your fears to Me, they are translated from the language of fear into the language of faith. And your faith in Me—and My love for you—will bless and keep you always.

Your loving Father

Forgiveness

Bear with each other and forgive whatever grievances you may have against one another. Forgive as the Lord forgave you.

Colossians 3:13

Forgive one another as quickly and thoroughly as God in Christ forgave you.

Ephesians 4:32 THE MESSAGE

Jesus said, "When you stand praying, if you hold anything against anyone, forgive him, so that your Father in heaven may forgive you your sins."

Mark 11:25

Peter came to Jesus and asked, "Lord, when my fellow believer sins against me, how many times must I forgive him? Should I forgive him as many as seven times?" Jesus answered, "I tell you, you must forgive him more than seven times. You must forgive him even if he does wrong to you seventy-seven times."

Matthew 18:21-22 NCV

A further reason for forgiveness is to keep from being outsmarted by Satan, for we know what he is trying to do.

2 Corinthians 2:11 TLB

NEVER GIVE UP

The old man rises from the evening meal and walks to the crest of the hill outside his dwelling, surveying the horizon. Squinting into the blaze of the setting sun, he shields his eyes and searches the landscape. Every day he comes, ever since his son left home.

He feels the sting of tears as he recalls the tender years of the boy's youth—the laughter and the love; the warmth of his embrace. But in recent years, the young man had thrust a dagger of disrespect into his old heart and twisted it with betrayal. He had taken his inheritance and left.

One of the young stewards approaches. "Why don't you quit torturing yourself like this, Sir? He isn't coming back."

The patriarch stands in silence for several minutes. Finally, he speaks. "I'll never give up; he's my son."

In that moment a distant silhouette appears against the sky. He strains to see. Suddenly, the great heart of the man seizes with recognition. It is his son—slumped, dirty, and dragging his feet—but his son all the same. The old man clutches at his chest and gasps at the crisp air. It isn't pain he feels; it's compassion. Gathering his heavy robes into his fists, he breaks and runs, galloping across the landscape with his gray hair streaming in the wind behind him. (See Luke 15:11-32).

When someone has broken trust, it's tempting to demand an apology, to put him on probation, to make her earn your trust again. But the wisdom of the prodigal's father defies human standards and forgives with scandalous grace—the grace of God. Go, and do likewise.

Freedom

Jesus answered, "Everyone who drinks this water will be thirsty again, but whoever drinks the water I give him will never thirst. Indeed, the water I give him will become in him a spring of water welling up to eternal life."

John 4:13-14

Jesus said, "If the Son makes you free, you will be free indeed."

John 8:36 RSV

We know that our old life died with Christ on the cross so that our sinful selves would have no power over us and we would not be slaves to sin. Anyone who has died is made free from sin's control.

Romans 6:6-7 NCV

Jesus said, "If you continue in my word, you are truly my disciples, and you will know the truth, and the truth will make you free."

John 8:31-32 RSV

Now you are free from the power of sin and are slaves of God, and his benefits to you include holiness and everlasting life.

Romans 6:22 TLB

THE WATER OF LIFE

"May I have a drink, Ma'am?" the stranger says, sitting down in the shade of a tall shrub.

"I can't believe You would stoop so low," she sneers. "You people would sooner die of thirst than ask someone like me for water."

"I suppose I should have offered you a drink then," He nods.

"You don't even have a water pot," she says, thinking she has the upper hand. "How are You going to offer me water?"

"I have water that is not from this well," He says, smiling. "I have water that will quench the relentless thirst that resides deep in your soul."

"What do you mean?" she asks, tipping her head slightly.

"I have the water of life," the stranger answers. He snaps a twig from the shrub and examines it closely. "Eternal life, that is. My living water will free you from your parched existence."

"Okay, if You say You have this living water, then give me some." She intended to call His bluff.

"First, go get your husband." There is silence as He twirls the twig between His fingers.

Finally she answers, "I don't have a husband."

"I know," Jesus rises from the ground and approaches her slowly. "And though you've had several, they have all been just like the man you are living with now—men who mistreat you, abuse you, and abandon you after awhile." He lifts the water pot from her arms. "I'm here to set you free from your burden of hopelessness." (See John 4:7-18).

What a wonderful freedom and wholeness comes from meeting Jesus right where you are and receiving the revelation of who He is!

Friendship

A friend loveth at all times.

Proverbs 17:17 KJV

As iron sharpens iron, a friend sharpens a friend.

Proverbs 27:17 NLT

The eye cannot say to the hand, "I have no need of you," nor again the
head to the feet, "I have no need of you." On the contrary, the parts of
the body which seem to be weaker are indispensable.

1 Corinthians 12:21-22 RSV

Jesus said, "This is my commandment, that you love one another
as I have loved you. No one has greater love than this,
to lay down one's life for one's friends."

John 15:12-13 NRSV

Disregarding another person's faults preserves love;
telling about them separates close friends.

Proverbs 17:9 NLT

Accept one another, then, just as Christ accepted you.

Romans 15:7

Heavenly Father,

I've always thought that friendship should be light and fun and lots of laughs. When one of my friends got serious on me, said something I didn't like, or expected too much from me, I just went in a different direction and found someone else to have fun with. Now, I look around and I don't like what I see. I'm not sure any of the people in my life really care about me, and I'm not sure I truly care about any of them.

Lord, I'm sorry for being so shallow and short-sighted. I do want friends whom I can care about deeply, who are there through thick and thin, who can tell me the hard things that make me a better person. And I want to become that kind of friend myself. Will You help me?

Amen.

A DIFFERENT KIND OF FRIEND

"Mom, I don't think my friendship with Allie is going to survive." Even though she was grown and married, Mindy liked to get her mother's take on things.

"Why, what happened?" Janie was stirring spaghetti sauce at the stove.

"It's just that I do things for her all the time, but she doesn't reciprocate," Mindy reached for a spoon and dipped it into the pot.

"What things?"

"Well . . . I call her all the time, but she rarely calls me. I ask her to lunch; I offer to go shopping with her, I go to the hairdresser with her, and I even make sure she gets invited to other people's parties. And what do I get?" she waved her spoon in a circular motion, "A big, fat zero!"

"Really?" Janie turned from the stove. "Isn't she the friend who always has a shoulder to cry on and a word of encouragement? Isn't Allie the one who is never moody, irritable, or impatient? And didn't you tell me she never gossips? In fact, didn't she come to your rescue the other day when you needed a sitter?"

"So, what's your point? She still doesn't call or shop; things like that."

"My point is that every individual has unique gifts to offer in a relationship. If you don't accept her way of loving, you are simply depriving yourself of the gift of her friendship."

"But she doesn't give in the ways I want her to," Mindy complained.

"Better yet, she gives in the ways you need for her to. Her friendship is a gift from God."

Do you properly value all the friends God has placed in your life?

My Precious Child,

Friendship is one of the most precious gifts on earth. You have robbed yourself of its blessings and benefits for too long, but it's never too late. If you really want strong, long-term friendships, you will need to learn how to be a good friend yourself.

Begin by working on your relationship with Me. In that way, you will see all the important characteristics of true friendship: love—selfless and giving; joy—in your friend's blessings as well as your own; peace—putting aside disagreements; patience—when your friend disappoints you; kindness; goodness; faithfulness; gentleness; and self-control. We'll work on all of them together. And while we're at it, you'll recognize those who are true friends—and they will recognize you.

Your loving Father

Generosity

It is good to be merciful and generous.
Those who are fair in their business
will never be defeated.
Good people will always be remembered.
Psalm 112:5-6 NCV

A generous man will prosper;
he who refreshes others will himself be refreshed.
Proverbs 11:25

Whoever sows sparingly will also reap sparingly, and whoever sows
generously will also reap generously. Each man should give what he has
decided in his heart to give, not reluctantly or under compulsion,
for God loves a cheerful giver.
2 Corinthians 9:6-7

Good men will be generous to others and
will be blessed of God for all they do.
Isaiah 32:8 TLB

If someone does wrong to you, do not pay him back by
doing wrong to him. ...Defeat evil by doing good.
Romans 12:17, 21 NCV

THE POSITIVE POWER OF GIVING

Mason had been waiting ten minutes and still no wait staff—no water. Finally, a young woman appeared, mopping her forehead with the back of her hand.

"What can I get you to drink?" she asked breathlessly.

"How about iced tea with lemon," Mason beamed.

Disappearing without a word, she returned after another ten minutes. "Sorry about the wait," she placed the tea in front of Mason. No lemon. "What do you want to eat?"

"What are your specials?" Mason inquired.

"They're posted out front," her tone was harsh, unfriendly.

"I think I'll just have a chef's salad with your house dressing," he folded his menu and offered it to the young woman. "Could you put the dressing on the side, please?"

She snatched the menu and walked away.

Another twenty minutes passed before the salad finally arrived—dressed. "Sorry about that," she said with monotone indifference. "The kitchen staff is incompetent, if you ask me." She left the ticket on the edge of the table, never to return.

Mason pulled a twenty-dollar bill from his wallet. "That's nine for the meal and eleven for the girl," he muttered to himself, "for whatever ails her."

As he approached the door, she yelled from behind him, "Sir!"

He turned to see her running toward him waving his change.

"My daughter is very ill and I took it out on you," tears were streaming down her face. "I can't accept this considering the way—"

"—you mean the way you blessed me with the opportunity to give?" He smiled and closed her fist over the money.

A truly generous person gives unconditionally.

Gentleness

My friends, if anyone is detected in a transgression, you who have received the Spirit should restore such a one in a spirit of gentleness. Take care that you yourselves are not tempted.

Galatians 6:1 NRSV

Are there those among you who are truly wise and understanding? Then they should show it by living right and doing good things with a gentleness that comes from wisdom.

James 3:13 NCV

A soft answer turns away wrath, but harsh words cause quarrels.

Proverbs 15:1 TLB

The Lord's servants must not quarrel but must be kind to everyone. They must be . . . patient with difficult people. They should gently teach those who oppose the truth. Perhaps God will change those people's hearts, and they will believe the truth. Then they will come to their senses and escape from the Devil's trap.

2 Timothy 2:24-26 NLT

Jesus said, "God blesses those who are gentle and lowly, for the whole earth will belong to them."

Matthew 5:5 NLT

CONSIDERING OPTIONS

Gentleness is easy when things are going smoothly and everyone is on track. But what about when someone is out of line and causing you grief? In Galatians 6:1, the apostle Paul wrote: "Brothers, if someone is caught in a sin, you who are spiritual should restore him gently."

Can you catch a vision for the meaning behind that Bible-talk? Consider this.

You are walking with several others down a narrow mountain pass alongside a steep incline. Wind and rain beat against your back, pressing you faster down the pathway than you want to go. Suddenly, the man immediately in front of you stumbles and slips over the ledge. Grasping the edge of the cliff, he is barely able to keep his grip.

Instantly, you lunge forward, grabbing hold of his wrists with both of your hands—you catch him in his fall! With your weight, you anchor him against the gravity that threatens to pull you both to your death.

On the precipice of disaster, the man panics. You speak to him with gentle words of encouragement: "Hang on, buddy, I've got you. You're gonna make it."

Once he is calm, you are able to dangle your head over the ledge and coach him where to place his feet. Together you inch him back onto the straight and narrow. Crisis averted—life saved.

Do you now catch Paul's appeal for gentleness? He isn't suggesting that you should condone the sin, or enable someone to continue in a wrong behavior. But he is saying that when we extend kindness and compassion, we are following God's example of goodness and grace.

God's Kingdom

Jesus said, "Turn from sin, and turn to God,
for the Kingdom of Heaven is near."
Matthew 4:17 TLB

Jesus said, "You will have complete and free access to God's kingdom,
keys to open any and every door: no more barriers between heaven
and earth, earth and heaven."
Matthew 16:19 THE MESSAGE

Jesus said, "Do not worry, saying, 'What will we eat?' or 'What will we
drink?' or 'What will we wear?' . . . Indeed your heavenly Father knows
that you need all these things. But strive first for the kingdom of God
and his righteousness, and all these things will be given to you as well."
Matthew 6:31-33 NRSV

You will joyfully give thanks to the Father who has made you able to have
a share in all that he has prepared for his people in the kingdom of light.
God has freed us from the power of darkness, and he brought us into
the kingdom of his dear Son.
Colossians 1:12-13 NCV

Jesus said, "The kingdom of God does not come with your careful
observation, nor will people say, 'Here it is,' or 'There it is,' because the
kingdom of God is within you."
Luke 17:20-21

Heavenly Father,

I can't help but imagine how different things will
be when Your kingdom becomes a physical reality.
When I shut my eyes, I think I can see it. All around
me people are shouting Your praises and dancing joyfully. There are no jails, no police, no criminals,
because Your kingdom is ruled by the law of love.
Peace is almost a tangible substance in the air, radiating from the Prince of Peace, who is seated on His
throne.

Lord, I want so much to be there, in a place where
all anxiety, heartache, pain, poverty, tragedy, cruelty,
chaos, and evil have been banished. Give me a patient
heart as I wait for that day, keeping the kernel of hope
deep in my heart.

Amen.

HE WILL WELCOME YOU

A man traveling from a distant land came upon a congregation of believers that he thought to be a small city. "Whom do you serve?" he asked the oldest among them.

"The Lord," the believer answered.

"What lord?" the stranger pressed, unable to detect the upper case "L" in his response.

"The Lord God Almighty, King of heaven and earth," the believer explained.

"Sounds like a tyrant, am I right?" the traveler inquired.

"No, He is compassionate, merciful, gracious, tenderhearted, forgiving, and loving."

"I'll bet he taxes you heavily, correct?" he persisted.

"No, not at all; but He encourages us to give freely and from our hearts as we are able," said the man from the congregation.

"But he takes your young men into bloody battles in order to expand his kingdom, doesn't he?" he looked perplexed.

"No, He takes young and old into His bosom to bring them into His safekeeping."

"Surely he requires that you give your life for him," the stranger continued.

"Actually, He laid down His life for us," the Christian responded.

A thoughtful pause lingered upon the traveler's mind.

"How can I become a citizen of this kingdom?" he asked.

"Simply consult the King—He will welcome you," the man answered with assurance.

"Where is his throne?" he inquired.

"Within us," the man answered.

The stranger stood, puzzling. He shuffled his feet in the dirt and shifted his cane from hand to hand. Finally he said, "I'm afraid I don't know how to find him."

"You needn't be anxious, Sir," the man smiled, "for He has already found you."

My Precious Child,

It will indeed be a wonderful day, when all My people come to join Me in My kingdom. I long for it just as you do. Still . . . I think you have forgotten something very important. My kingdom is not a vague concept without power or substance, where you will spend eternity. My kingdom is real and accessible to you at all times.

When you feel lonely—reach inside for My comfort and companionship. When you feel anxious—reach inside for My peace. When you feel sad and cast down—reach inside for My joy. I have placed My kingdom in the hearts of My people. Yes. It's inside of you. And you can live there even now.

Your loving Father

God's Love

God shows his great love for us in this way:
Christ died for us while we were still sinners.

Romans 5:8 NCV

The LORD passed in front of Moses and said, "I am the LORD.
The LORD is a God who shows mercy, who is kind, who doesn't become
angry quickly, who has great love and faithfulness and
is kind to thousands of people. The LORD forgives people for evil,
for sin, and for turning against him."

Exodus 34:6-7 NCV

They refused to listen;
they forgot the miracles you did for them.
So they became stubborn and turned against you,
choosing a leader to take them back to slavery.
But you are a forgiving God.
You are kind and full of mercy.
You do not become angry quickly, and you have great love.
So you did not leave them.

Nehemiah 9:17 NCV

The LORD shows mercy and is kind.
He does not become angry quickly, and he has great love.

Psalm 103:8 NCV

NO STRINGS ATTACHED

On the night of betrayal, Judas led a band of Roman soldiers to Jesus in Gethsemane, expecting that He would try to evade capture. But instead, He volunteered to go. This was the first of many surprises the soldiers would encounter that night as they attempted to round up the motley group of insurgents and their unorthodox leader.

The second surprise must have been the impassioned response of one of Jesus' disciples. In an attempt to defend his Master, Peter struck one of the Romans with his sword. Aiming for his head, he missed and lopped off an ear. Can you imagine what must have gone through that man's mind when he reached up and felt only blood spurting from the gaping hole on the side of his head? Yet more profound must have been his experience when Jesus, offering a mild rebuke to Peter, reached down and retrieved the piece of flesh from the ground, pressing it back into place and healing it completely. The holy palm of the Lord rested with warmth and concern against the face of the foreigner who was trying to take him by force.

Why would this man reach with compassion to heal another who intended Him harm? Because the love of the Almighty had complete possession of His heart. And simply put, the mercies of heaven make no earthly sense.

The love of God is indiscriminate. He embraces not only those who reciprocate, but also those who rebel and betray Him. There is nothing in this world that can separate you from the love of God. It is His gift—unconditional and with no strings attached.

God's Presence

The Lord had said through the prophet: "The virgin will be with child
and will give birth to a son, and they will call him Immanuel"
—which means, "God with us."

Matthew 1:22-23

Jesus said, "Where two or three are gathered together in my name,
there am I in the midst of them."

Matthew 18:20 KJV

Jesus said, "I am with you always, to the close of the age."

Matthew 28:20 RSV

Where can I flee from your presence?
If I rise on the wings of the dawn,
if I settle on the far side of the sea,
even there your hand will guide me,
your right hand will hold me fast.

Psalm 139:7, 9-10

Blessed are those who have learned to acclaim you,
who walk in the light of your presence, O LORD.

Psalm 89:15

UNEXPECTED PLACES

"Surely the LORD is in this place, and I was not aware of it" (Genesis 28:16). Jacob spoke those words after he awakened from a dream about a stairway reaching to heaven. At the top of the stairs stood the Lord. Angels were ascending and descending upon the ladder, carrying the burdens of faithful men into the throne room and bringing blessings back in response.

Banished from home, Jacob was running from death threats made by his brother. It must have seemed like a strange place to encounter the Almighty.

God has a history of showing up in unexpected places and in unbelievable circumstances. He hovers over the lives of His people with a watchful eye and a heart of understanding. Thus, when you least expect Him, when you think you least deserve a visit from on high, He appears to bless you with affirmation and assurance.

Thousands of years after Jacob's dream, a man named Nathanael stood under a fig tree in Israel, contemplating things that had stirred in his heart at the preaching of John the Baptist. Those private thoughts held deep significance for him.

The Lord appeared to him—Jesus, the long-awaited Messiah. Nathanael was skeptical. There had been many false claims of messiahship.

"When you were under the fig tree, I saw you," Jesus assured him.

"How could You know my deepest thoughts unless You are the very Son of God?" Nathanael exclaimed.

"You shall see the heavens opened, and the angels of God ascending and descending on the Son of Man," He answered. (See John 1:48-51).

The God who once stood at the top of the stairs has come down from heaven. The presence of God is in your midst.

God's Will

Be joyful always; pray continually; give thanks in all circumstances,
for this is God's will for you in Christ Jesus.

1 Thessalonians 5:16-18

Do not conform any longer to the pattern of this world,
but be transformed by the renewing of your mind.
Then you will be able to test and approve what God's will is
—his good, pleasing and perfect will.

Romans 12:2

The Holy Spirit helps us with our daily problems and in our praying.
For we don't even know what we should pray for nor how to pray as we
should, but the Holy Spirit . . . pleads for us in harmony with
God's own will.

Romans 8:26-27 TLB

Jesus said, "Take my yoke upon you, and learn from me;
for I am gentle and humble in heart, and you will find rest for your
souls. For my yoke is easy, and my burden is light."

Matthew 11:29-30 NRSV

God's commands are not too hard for us.

1 John 5:3 NCV

Heavenly Father,

I used to think that following Your will for my life would mean losing my own will, giving up the things I love to do, becoming another person. I honestly thought I might end up somewhere far from home doing something I didn't want to do. Now I know that just the opposite is true. As I surrender to Your will, my own is enhanced and purified and allowed to grow and bloom. For that, I'm so grateful, Lord.

Once again, I offer You all that I am and ever hope to be. I take pleasure in the purposes for which You created me. Open my heart to expose every thought and feeling that is not in harmony with Your will. I want my life to be fully vested in eternity, to be without reluctance, without hesitation, Your vessel.

Amen.

WHAT GOD WANTS

God's will for you is joy!

When you come to know the Lord—really know Him—you gain a new perspective on joy. This new joy is derived from the intimacy you share with Jesus rather than from the ease and abundance of your circumstances, which were most likely the criteria for your pre-Jesus joy. In fact, if you walk closely with the Lord, you may find that you actually cherish the lean times and tough situations because of the growth you experience as you exercise your faith. If you want to know joy, you must really know Jesus. If you come to know Jesus, joy is inevitable.

God's will for you is prayer!

A high-level consciousness of the presence of God results in continual prayer. The dynamic, interpersonal relationship you develop reorients your mind and your heart to dwell upon Him, to be more aware of Him, to anticipate Him. Continual prayer means keeping the counsel of the Almighty always at hand. Making inquiry of the Lord in every circumstance. Listening for His response.

God's will for you is thanksgiving!

You would agree, no doubt, that giving thanks is effortless in the good times—but it isn't easy in every circumstance. But being easy isn't the point; being necessary is. Gratitude in your heart and on your lips is the bold confession of the sovereignty of God. In your expression of thanks, God reigns. His power is accessed and applied through your grateful response to every circumstance.

Joy, prayer, thanksgiving—God wills what's best for you!

My Precious Child,

I have so many plans for you. Wonderful plans. But I give you My word, I won't ask you to do anything that you don't want to do. I meant it when I said that you've been given a "free" will. That's why I'm committed to wait until you make the decision to place yourself in My hands. Even then, we'll look at each new decision together. You will always have time to think it over and choose for yourself.

Within My creation, there are many who are compelled to do My bidding—the angels for example. But that is not the case with you. It was My desire to give you freedom to choose to love and obey Me. I promise you this: if you surrender your will to Mine, I will see to it that you have everything you need to fulfill all those wonderful plans I have for you.

Your loving Father

God's Word

The Word that God speaks is alive and full of power [making it active, operative, energizing, and effective]; it is sharper than any two-edged sword, penetrating to the dividing line of the breath of life . . . and . . . spirit, and . . . [of the deepest parts of our nature], exposing and sifting and analyzing and judging the very thoughts and purposes of the heart.

Hebrews 4:12 AMP

The Word became flesh and made his dwelling among us.
We have seen his glory, the glory of the One and Only,
who came from the Father, full of grace and truth.

John 1:14

Your word is a lamp for my feet
and a light for my path.

Psalm 119:105 NLT

Your words are what sustain me; they are food to my hungry soul.
They bring joy to my sorrowing heart and delight me.

Jeremiah 15:16 TLB

I treasure your word in my heart,
so that I may not sin against you.

Psalm 119:11 NRSV

FULL OF TRUTH

The Word lives! It comes to life within you when you read or listen to it, and it breathes into your soul the essence of God. You see your own life written in the pages of the book, and you find that the book has been written into your life. It inspires, vivifies, and invigorates the deadness in your heart, bringing you to your faithful feet and to the fullness of your stature in Christ.

The Word is active! It is not passive, dormant, idle, or impotent. It is engaged within your mind, moving within your heart, working within your world, effective within your relationships, progressive within your vision, productive within your actions, and powerful upon your outcome. The Word is dynamic!

The Word is full of grace! It softens you, forgives you, heals you, comforts you, guides you, encourages you, enlightens you, and transforms you.

The Word is full of truth! It convicts you of sin, convinces you of your need for Jesus, conforms your thinking to a spiritual standard, and transforms your mind into the likeness of the Lord. It is powerful, liberating, effective, and eternal.

The Bible is the Word of God. It has been written to you by Almighty God just as one would write a letter to a loved one. It's a personal matter, written in a way that gives comfort, purpose, and clarity to every area of your life. Read it often and let its transforming power renew and restore your heart and mind.

Goodness

Whenever you are able,
do good to people who need help.
Proverbs 3:27 NCV

The Kingdom of God is not a matter of what we eat or drink,
but of living a life of goodness and peace and joy in the Holy Spirit.
If you serve Christ with this attitude, you will please God.
Romans 14:17-18 NLT

In the past you were full of darkness, but now you are full of light in the
Lord. So live like children who belong to the light. Light brings every
kind of goodness, right living, and truth.
Ephesians 5:8-9 NCV

If you are wise and understand God's ways,
live a life of steady goodness so that only good deeds will pour forth.
James 3:13 NLT

You were made free from sin, and now you are slaves to goodness.
Romans 6:18 NCV

Heavenly Father,

I want to be a good person—like You. That's why I try so hard to do good things. But somehow, Lord, I think there must be more to it. It seems to me that being good is a condition rather than a behavior, something that radiates from the inside out. Until that happens, I think I will always feel like a phony, doing without being.

I offer my heart to You, Lord. I ask You to transform my soul. Make it sensitive to the needs of others—like You were when You walked here on earth. Make it wise and able to see what is in another's best interest. Make it gracious enough to reach out to those who cannot reciprocate. Most of all, make me good in the same way You are good—to the core and always in harmony with eternal purposes.

Amen.

ALL THE WAY

Glenda Ross hurried through the parking lot of a busy super-store two nights before Christmas. People were everywhere—tired, frustrated, and rushed. Glenda wheeled her cart through the lot, slipping and sliding as she went, to the far end of the row of parked cars.

There she saw a distinguished old man sitting on the icy pavement, inching along on his hindquarters, with a rather frumpy old woman sitting in his lap facing forward. Glenda was startled at the sight of them. "Uh, excuse me, Sir," she blurted out. "What's going on?"

He chuckled and his eyes sparkled up at her. "Well, I was headed for the store when I happened upon this nice lady. She had fallen on the ice."

"Oh, my!" Glenda interjected.

"I couldn't get her up," the man continued, "and I sure couldn't just leave her there in that short coat. So since I have long britches, I sat down where she could roll on my lap like I was a wagon. I figured I'd just have to scoot her to her car. Sure couldn't let her freeze to death."

"Sir, you won't have any britches left if you scoot her all the way to her car," Glenda said, stifling an amazed giggle.

"I suppose I'd rather be a man without britches than a man without a heart," he grinned and winked.

Glenda helped them both up and to their respective places—realizing she'd just seen goodness in action.

True goodness is more than the absence of what is bad. It's proactive, always looking for ways to express itself. It is a by-product of a relationship with God.

My Precious Child,

You're right to think that you have no power to be "good" on your own. Your natural instinct is to take your selfless action and somehow turn it to your own advantage. There is only one way to triumph. That is to have My nature implanted into your heart through the power of the Holy Spirit. Once that has been done, the seeds of goodness will begin to grow and blossom within you.

Don't worry, My child. I understand your limitations, and I applaud your efforts, flawed though they may be. Know that I'm committed to helping you become like Me in every way. All it takes on your part is a willingness to invite My Spirit to take over and do within you what you cannot do for yourself.

Your loving Father

Grace

Now God has us where he wants us, with all the time in this world and
the next to shower grace and kindness upon us in Christ Jesus.

Ephesians 2:7 THE MESSAGE

From his fullness we have all received, grace upon grace. The law indeed
was given through Moses; grace and truth came through Jesus Christ.

John 1:16-17 NRSV

The amazing grace of the Master, Jesus Christ, the extravagant love of
God, the intimate friendship of the Holy Spirit, be with all of you.

2 Corinthians 13:14 THE MESSAGE

If your life honors the name of Jesus, he will honor you.
Grace is behind and through all of this, our God giving himself freely,
the Master, Jesus Christ, giving himself freely.

2 Thessalonians 1:12 THE MESSAGE

Even though on the outside it often looks like things are falling apart
on us, on the inside, where God is making new life,
not a day goes by without his unfolding grace.

2 Corinthians 4:16 THE MESSAGE

GOD'S GOODNESS AND FAVOR

The grace of God is His goodness and favor poured out on us. The Bible account of the lame man Jesus encountered at the Sheep Gate pool in Jerusalem is a good example (John 5:1-15):

1. Grace is indiscriminate. The invalid lying at the pool had been in that condition for thirty-eight years. In man's estimation, he was a nobody with nothing to offer.

2. Grace takes the initiative. Upon seeing him, Jesus made the first move, "'Do you want to get well?'"

3. Grace is not dependent upon understanding. The man thought Jesus was speaking about the healing power of the pool. He had no idea that He was the Healer.

4. Grace inspires obedience. Jesus issued an irresistible command: "Get up! Pick up your mat and walk." No doubt it was the most thrilling thing the man had ever been ordered to do.

5. Grace does its greatest work through the most glaring insufficiency. The man's infirmity—that which kept him from functioning in society—was completely remedied.

6. Grace is scandalous. It was the Sabbath, and when the man picked up his mat to carry it, he was in violation of the religious traditions of his day.

7. Grace confronts ignorance and unbelief. He had been so carried away with the gift that he had neglected to know the Giver.

8. Grace is a discipline. Jesus found him again and cautioned him to stop sinning—to live worthy of the gift he had received.

9. Grace demands a witness. The man publicly proclaimed that it was Jesus who had healed him.
   God wants to reveal the mystery of His grace in your life.

Grief

Very truly, I tell you, you will weep and mourn, but the world will
rejoice; you will have pain, but your pain will turn into joy.

John 16:20 NRSV

The LORD is close to the brokenhearted
and saves those who are crushed in spirit.

Psalm 34:18

When my heart was grieved
and my spirit embittered,
I was senseless and ignorant;
I was a brute beast before you.
Yet I am always with you;
you hold me by my right hand.

Psalm 73:21-23

Jesus said, "Blessed are those who mourn,
For they shall be comforted."

Matthew 5:4 NKJV

Heavenly Father,

My heart is breaking. It feels as if I've lost everything—my hope, my courage, my joy, my life. The hurt presses on my chest until it's difficult to breathe. Surely, the feeble, ghostly voice that comes out of my mouth belongs to someone else. My legs seem quite unable to support my body. My friends gather around. They mean well, but their words seem hollow and empty. They can't possibly comprehend my loss. I feel cut off, isolated, ruined.

I offer all that is left of me—and that seems like very little—to You as a sacrificial gift of praise, my Lord. Take my exhausted body, my numb emotions, my salty tears, and help me release the burden of my grief into Your waiting arms.

Amen.

THE STAIN OF SALTY TEARS

A funeral procession heads toward the cemetery at the edge of a small town in Israel. The heavy footfall of a woman follows just behind the casket containing the lifeless body of her only son. With one hand extended, she holds to the edge of the bier, while with the other she clutches the garment which covers her heart. Already widowed, she is burying her only reason for living. Her great sorrow pours down her cheeks in rivers of salty tears.

A stranger stands just off the beaten path observing her grief. He tilts His head slightly in contemplation of His own imminent death and the grief His own dear mother will soon be asked to endure. A familiar ache swells inside, throbbing within His chest like the constant beating of a funeral drum—a longing to relieve the sorrow mothers feel when their children die.

As He approaches the pallbearers, He stretches out His hand to halt their monotonous progress. Suddenly aware, she looks up to see the source of the stall. There He stands, so close she can see her reflection in His compassionate eyes.

Her gaze moves from His face to the young man lying upon the bier, and slowly back again. A torrent of tears washes the strength from under her attempt to give voice to her words. He nods, knowingly, and turns to the coffin. Nudging the boy on the shoulder, He says, "Get up, Son, your mother is crying." And astonishingly, he does. (See Luke 7:11-17).

This mother and son were eventually separated again by death. But when you are reunited with your loved one in heavenly places—the celebration will last for eternity.

My Precious Child,

I see your tears. I hear your sobs—those that can be heard by human ears and those that cannot. Take My hand, and together we will walk through the hours, weeks, and months ahead.

I promise to be there when you need Me the most, and also when you need Me the least. That means that I will be there for you "always." I will never leave you. I am aware of every tortured breath, every painful regret, every angry thought—and I'm here to comfort and uphold you.

Slowly but surely I will restore your hope and return the song to your heart. Though you can't believe it now—one day you will live again, laugh again, love again. One day you will wake up and find that your salty tears have been transformed to joy unspeakable and full of glory.

Your loving Father

Guilt

If we claim to be without sin, we deceive ourselves and the truth is not in us. If we confess our sins, he is faithful and just and will forgive us our sins and purify us from all unrighteousness.

1 John 1:8-9

There was a time when I wouldn't admit what a sinner I was. But my dishonesty made me miserable and filled my days with frustration. All day and all night your hand was heavy on me. My strength evaporated like water on a sunny day until I finally admitted all my sins to you and stopped trying to hide them. I said to myself, "I will confess them to the Lord." And you forgave me! All my guilt is gone.

Psalm 32:3-5 TLB

As far as the east is from the west, so far has he removed our transgressions from us.

Psalm 103:12

What happiness for those whose guilt has been forgiven! What joys when sins are covered over! What relief for those who have confessed their sins and God has cleared their record.

Psalm 32:1-2 TLB

DEEP WATERS

A surefire path to a guilt-ridden conscience is denial. That's correct—lie to yourself and to everyone else, and you'll be a miserable person inside. Deny that you have sinned, refuse to admit your failings, and renounce the truth about your fall, and you'll never trust anyone else, either. But be aware, the barricade of self-deception that you construct within your heart will hold only a little while, probably as long as the tide of accusation swells. Once the storm has passed, the wall of defense starts to crumble, and the deep waters of guilt start to seep through.

Do you want to know a bona fide cure for guilt? Confess your trespass, acknowledge your mistakes, and own up to your lapse in judgment. God is so gracious, He will forgive you faster than you can finish repenting. In fact, He is so compassionate that He starts the healing before the words fall from your lips. The Lord is such a faithful Friend that He will rush to stand in as the witness to your righteousness. Jesus is such an understanding Savior that He covers you when you are vulnerable to keep you from unmerciful exposure.

God cleanses the heart, restores the relationship, and washes away the stains of guilt. Do you want to be free from guilt? Be truthful with others, with God, and most of all, with yourself.

Holy Spirit

We have not received the spirit of the world but the Spirit who is from God, that we may understand what God has freely given us. This is what we speak, not in words taught us by human wisdom but in words taught by the Spirit, expressing spiritual truths in spiritual words.

1 Corinthians 2:12-13

Jesus said, "When the Father sends the Counselor as my representative— and by the Counselor I mean the Holy Spirit—he will teach you every- thing and will remind you of everything I myself have told you."

John 14:26 NLT

I keep asking that the God of our Lord Jesus Christ . . . may give you the Spirit of wisdom and revelation, so that you may know him better.

Ephesians 1:17

Jesus said, "I will send you the Comforter-the Holy Spirit, the source of all truth. He will come to you from the Father and will tell you all about me."

John 15:26 TLB

Jesus said, "I will ask the Father, and he will give you another Counselor, who will never leave you. He is the Holy Spirit, who leads into all truth."

John 14:16-17 NLT

DESPERATE HEARTS—DEEPER DIMENSIONS

There are things you can know about God with your mind—information related to creation, covenant, miracles, prophecies, promises, and the like. Any historian may cite the details of the biblical record with impeccable accuracy. But the things you know about God with your heart—His love, mercy, compassion, comfort, guidance, assurance, and hope—can only be known through His Spirit. The deep things of God are revealed by the Spirit who searches them out and reveals them to you.

For instance, when you read the Bible story about Jesus and the leper in Matthew 8, it is with your mind that you discover His power to heal. But it is through the Spirit that you feel the compassion of His touch upon your own desperate heart and understand His love in a deeper dimension—a love that heals the broken places in your life.

But revelation is only part of the Spirit's role. That which embodied and empowered Jesus as He touched the leper is the same Spirit indwelling you and empowering you to live the Spirit-filled life. Imparting wisdom to touch the hearts of others with His compassion and love, as well, you transmit healing grace with power when you demonstrate what you've received.

First, a revelation by the Spirit; then the wisdom of the Spirit to act on what was revealed and create change. That's how the Holy Spirit works in the lives of those who are God's children. That's how the Holy Spirit can and will work in your life.

Hope

May the God of hope fill you with all joy and peace in believing,
so that by the power of the Holy Spirit you may abound in hope.

Romans 15:13 RSV

The LORD looks after those who fear him,
those who put their hope in his love.
He saves them from death
and spares their lives in times of hunger.

Psalm 33:18-19 NCV

Against all hope, Abraham in hope believed and so became
the father of many nations, just as it had been said to him,
"So shall your offspring be."

Romans 4:18

The LORD is good to those whose hope is in him,
to the one who seeks him.

Lamentations 3:25

Be strong and take courage,
all you who put your hope in the LORD!

Psalm 31:24 NLT

Heavenly Father,

I just want to thank You for bringing hope to my life. When the bills come pouring in but the money doesn't, when my body isn't working like it should but the doctor can't seem to find anything wrong, when all the sundry storms of life blow me to and fro and rain on my parade, I find hope in the fact that we are family—You and I. That relationship gives me something to hang on to during the hard times.

Thank You, Lord, for the promise of a future hope—one that is greater and more wonderful than I could ever imagine. It is a hope that one day I will dwell securely among the riches of Your heavenly kingdom. All my troubles gone for good. Oh, what a day that will be!

Amen.

IF YOU HAD BEEN HERE

The sisters of Lazarus—Mary and Martha—send for Jesus when their brother falls ill (John 11). Because he and Jesus are close friends, they believe that Jesus will drop what He is doing and come at once. But that doesn't happen. Out in the hills of Galilee where He is teaching those who will listen about the love of God, Jesus tells His disciples to relax. "This sickness will not end in death," He tells them, "but will result in the glory of God."

The delay is long, but Jesus stays where He is until every person has been ministered to—then He summons His disciples, and they head for Bethany.

When the Lord and His followers finally arrive in Bethany, Lazarus has been in the tomb for four days.

Martha runs to meet him. "Lord!" she cries, "it would have been different if You had been here. I had hoped that You would heal him."

"Martha," Jesus consoles, "you must hope for more."

"Lord," Martha responds, "I know to hope for his resurrection at the last day."

"Hope must exist in the here and now. It must penetrate your weak faith and bring you to trust in the power of God," Jesus answers. "Don't rest your hope in healing—hope in Me."

A few moments later, Jesus calls Lazarus's name, and he walks out of the tomb in his grave clothes.

On that day, Martha learned what we all must learn—to place her hope and trust in a living, breathing Savior rather than in the outcome she is hoping for.

My Precious Child,

It's true! One day you will dwell in the mansion I've prepared for you. Every need will be met. Your body will no longer experience the ravages of age and illness. It will be perfect and whole. All will be well with you when you come to dwell with Me in My heavenly kingdom. You are right to place your hope in that.

Your hope, however, should not be confined to some day in the future. I am also the God of the "now." I am here to meet your need—now! I am here to touch and heal your body—now! I am here for you in trouble—now! Call on Me and place your hope in My faithfulness both now and in the future.

Your loving Father

Humility

I say, through the grace given unto me, to every man that is among you, not to think of himself more highly than he ought to think; but to think soberly, according as God hath dealt to every man the measure of faith.

Romans 12:3 KJV

Humble yourselves before the Lord and he will exalt you.

James 4:10 RSV

All of you serve each other with humble spirits, for God gives special blessings to those who are humble, but sets himself against those who are proud. If you will humble yourselves under the mighty hand of God, in his good time he will lift you up.

1 Peter 5:5-6 TLB

Toward the scorners he is scornful,
but to the humble he shows favor.

Proverbs 3:34 NRSV

All who humble themselves before the Lord shall be given
every blessing and shall have wonderful peace.

Psalm 37:11 TLB

EXPECTING NOTHING IN RETURN

Consider how many disagreements you have encountered over someone's insistence upon having his or her way. How many marriages have disintegrated because of a high-handed arrogance and lack of consideration? How many friendships have ended over pride and an unforgiving heart?

Now bring it a little closer to home. How often do you demand to be the one who chooses the restaurant? How upset are you when interruptions come your way? How hospitable are you, especially to those who have young children? How agreeable are you when your television program isn't chosen? How irritated do you appear to those who inconvenience you? How pleasant are you when you don't get the rest you "need"?

One person said, "Humility doesn't mean thinking lowly of yourself; it means being free of the need to consider yourself at all."

Take this challenge: For one week, expecting nothing in return.

· Serve someone else their coffee, tea, juice, milk, etc.
· Take out the trash.
· Park at the end of the aisle.
· Allow someone to go ahead of you in the checkout lane.
· Tip more than is required.
· Get up or arrive earlier to help someone else get started.
· Do someone's most dreaded chore.
· Help an elderly neighbor, aunt, parent, etc., with something that needs to be done.
· Pay the tab for someone who is eating alone.

Be creative about forgetting yourself. It could be fun! You might even find that being humble is the abundant life. Jesus did!

Identity

You are a chosen people, a royal priesthood, a holy nation,
a people belonging to God, that you may declare the praises of him who
called you out of darkness into his wonderful light.

1 Peter 2:9

Thus says the LORD,
he who created you, O Jacob,
he who formed you, O Israel:
"Fear not, for I have redeemed you;
I have called you by name, you are mine."

Isaiah 43:1 RSV

Jesus said, "You didn't choose me! I chose you!
I appointed you to go and produce lovely fruit always."

John 15:16 TLB

Jesus said, "You are the light that gives light to the world. . . .
Live so that they will see the good things you do and will praise your
Father in heaven."

Matthew 5:14,16 NCV

You are a people set apart as holy to GOD, your God.
GOD, your God, chose you out of all the people on Earth
for himself as a cherished, personal treasure.

Deuteronomy 7:6 THE MESSAGE

YOU ARE HIS

Do you remember how it felt to be chosen for the sandlot baseball team, the last dance at prom, the citizenship award at school? One little boy, arriving home from the first day of school, burst through the door waving a certificate and shouting with unrestrained joy: "Mom, I was chosen as the 'Very Best Walker in the Hall!'"

You have been chosen as part of a unique community of faithful people. Your identity is shaped by the character of the One who chose you. You have received a high calling for the fulfillment of a special purpose.

You are a priest. Your new identity stands you in the gap of intercession for those who do not know God or cannot muster the faith to approach Him. You are privileged to pray for those needing deliverance, healing, hope, joy, friendship, love, and most of all, Jesus.

You are holy. You reflect the glorious character of the Holy One upon the tarnished world in which you live. You radiate love, joy, peace, patience, kindness, goodness, faithfulness, gentleness, and self-control.

You are His. You are the cherished possession of the Almighty *Abba*. You occupy a special place in His heart, on His lap, in His house, in His family, and in His kingdom.

Your vocation is praise. You are a witness to the love and grace of God. You will not shut up or give up until you have held up the love of the Lord for all who will hear.

Integrity

Jesus said, "'You are a good and loyal servant. Because you were loyal
with small things, I will let you care for much greater things.
Come and share my joy with me.'"

Matthew 25:21 NCV

To the faithful you show yourself faithful;
to those with integrity you show integrity.

Psalm 18:25 NLT

The LORD does not look at the things man looks at.
Man looks at the outward appearance, but the LORD looks at the heart.

1 Samuel 16:7

I will be careful to live a blameless life . . .
I will lead a life of integrity
in my own home.

Psalm 101:2 NLT

Happy are people of integrity,
who follow the law of the LORD.
They do not compromise with evil,
and they walk only in his paths.

Psalm 119:1,3 NLT

Heavenly Father,

When the right thing is so easy to see, I don't understand why it can be so difficult to do—even the little things like not telling a white lie or pointing out the error when a merchant has given me too much change. But still, I stand there, shifting my weight from one foot to the other, point and counterpoint going on in my head. Why can't I just go ahead and do what I know I should do?

Lord, help me to settle the issue deep in my heart and make a full commitment to act as You would act, doing the right thing just because it's right. I feel that when my heart is settled, my mind will be too. No more rehearsing the facts or reviewing the consequences—just good old-fashioned honesty and integrity.

Amen.

THE CORRUPTIBLE HEART

Beliefs or values may be merely a "head" issue, while integrity is, without exception, a "heart" issue. The right words often come from the head, while the right actions usually come from the heart. That explains why we often hear people "talk the talk," yet fail to "walk the walk." In other words, your beliefs and values help you begin what integrity gives you the strength to finish, especially when your values are put to the test.

King Saul was a man with correct beliefs, but he had a corruptible heart. As long as he was esteemed by the people as the ultimate hero in Israel, he acted like a great leader. He was even willing to put his own life at risk for his subjects as long as they fed his pride. But when he was challenged by the shepherd boy whose faith was demonstrated in a heart of courage, Saul became a murdering maniac. He despised his most loyal devotee and stalked him relentlessly, trying to execute him for the bravery that had earned him popularity among the people.

Saul's struggle with integrity is potentially a struggle within the hearts of all. You might convince yourself that you hold firmly to a set of beliefs, but when your popularity, position, power, proximity, or pride is threatened, your values may suddenly be subordinated to your selfish impulses and desires; and you could compromise your integrity by the actions you take.

Take care to exercise your values in small matters so that you will have the spiritual muscle to demonstrate true integrity when the real contest comes.

My Precious Child,

You struggle because you have attached your integrity to a behavior. Attach it instead to a person—Me. Instruct your heart to do the right thing because it is pleasing to Me—your heavenly Father, who loves you more than life itself. You'll find that all the debate, all the posturing, all the excuses will evaporate, and you will feel the strength of conviction you need to handle the situation properly.

On your own, you are ill-equipped to live a life of integrity, but with the help of My Holy Spirit, who resides within you, you will emerge a winner in each contest—great or small. I have not called you to a life of frustration and failure. I've called you to be a victor, an overcomer.

Your loving Father

Jesus Christ

The Son is the radiance of God's glory and
the exact representation of his being.

Hebrews 1:3

Now we rejoice in our wonderful new relationship with God
—all because of what our Lord Jesus Christ has done
in dying for our sins—making us friends of God.

Romans 5:11 TLB

There is but one God, the Father, from whom all things came and for
whom we live; and there is but one Lord, Jesus Christ, through whom
all things came and through whom we live.

1 Corinthians 8:6

Jesus Christ is the same yesterday and today and for ever.

Hebrews 13:8 RSV

Jesus said, "I am the good shepherd; I know my own sheep,
and they know me, just as my Father knows me and I know the Father.
And I lay down my life for the sheep."

John 10:14-15 NLT

Jesus Christ rescued us from this evil world we're in by
offering himself as a sacrifice for our sins.

Galatians 1:4 THE MESSAGE

WHO IS THIS MAN?

The Jesus who unwittingly healed the hemorrhaging woman is an intentional revelation of God's compassion over your bleeding heart.

The Jesus who restored sight to the blind beggar is a glimpse afforded you into God's willingness to enlighten the eyes of your heart.

The Jesus who fed multitudes of strangers discloses for your sake the generosity of God's provision.

The Jesus who sat listening and talking to Mary one busy afternoon unveils to you the longing God has to interact with you in prayer.

The Jesus who wept with Martha and Mary at Lazarus's tomb tells the truth about God's sorrow over your grief.

The Jesus who held little children in His arms to bless them reveals to you the tender heart of your Father.

The Jesus who squatted in the dirt to draw attention away from a scantily clothed woman who was being exploited by religious arrogance exposes the way God protects your dignity and covers your sin.

The Jesus who raised the dead shows the power of the God who will resurrect you on the last day.

The Jesus who pleaded on behalf of His betrayers, "Forgive them, for they do not know what they are doing," demonstrates God's willingness to forgive you.

And the Jesus who laid down His life reveals to you the lavish grace of God and scandalous love with which you have been blessed.

Joy

You have endowed him with eternal happiness.
You have given him the unquenchable joy of your presence.

Psalm 21:6 TLB

Jesus said, "I have obeyed my Father's commands, and I remain in his
love. In the same way, if you obey my commands, you will remain in my
love. I have told you these things so that you can have the same joy I have
and so that your joy will be the fullest possible joy."

John 15:10-11 NCV

You have not seen Christ, but still you love him. You cannot see him
now, but you believe in him. So you are filled with a joy that cannot be
explained, a joy full of glory.

1 Peter 1:8 NCV

Salvation comes from God. What joys he gives to all his people.

Psalm 3:8 TLB

I'm whistling, laughing, and jumping for joy;
I'm singing your song, High God.

Psalm 9:2 THE MESSAGE

HEY, LOOK AT ME!

It is 3:00 in the afternoon. A crippled man lies begging at the gate of the temple at the time of prayer. As Peter and John approach, he asks them for money. They stop to look at the man.

This is awkward, the lame man thinks. *No one ever looks at me.*

The cripple, growing uncomfortable, dodges their gaze—looking beyond them to inquire of other passersby.

"Look at me!" Peter says.

Thinking they must intend to give him something substantial, he looks up.

Peter's voice is full of compassion, "I don't have any money, but what I do have, I give you gladly. In the name of Jesus Christ, walk!"

Without warning, Peter takes hold of the beggar's right hand, hoisting him up and onto his feet. Stunned by Peter's initiative and astonished to feel that his feet and ankles are steady beneath him, he stands aright. He then walks a step or two, springing up and down to see just how sturdy they are. He walks several circles around Peter and John, beaming, "Do you see this? I'm walking!"

The man cannot believe it. Overwhelmed with wonder, he follows the healers into the temple, walking, jumping, and praising the Lord. "Hey, look! Look at me! I have been crippled my whole life, and these two guys just asked Jesus to give me my legs! Is God good, or what?!"

His joy begs the attention of everyone in the temple courts, for no one else is praising the Lord. (See Acts 3:1-10).

When you understand the wonder of what God has done for you, there will be no restraining your joy—you will leap and shout and praise the Lord!

Knowing God

I want to know Christ and the power of his resurrection and
the fellowship of sharing in his sufferings, becoming like him in his
death, and so, somehow, to attain to the resurrection from the dead.

Philippians 3:10-11

This is how we may discern [daily, by experience] that we are coming to
know Him [to perceive, recognize, understand, and become better
acquainted with Him]: if we keep (bear in mind, observe, practice)
His teachings (precepts, commandments).

1 John 2:3 AMP

Dear friends, let us love one another, for love comes from God.
Everyone who loves has been born of God and knows God.

1 John 4:7

Jesus said, This is eternal life: [it means] to know (to perceive, recognize,
become acquainted with, and understand) You, the only true
and real God, and [likewise] to know Him, Jesus [as the] Christ
(the Anointed one, the Messiah), Whom You have sent.

John 17:3 AMP

In the past you did not know God. You were slaves to gods that were not
real. But now you know the true God. Really, it is God who knows you.

Galatians 4:8-9 NCV

TO KNOW HIM

If you want to . . .

Know Christ, there is one sure way: spend time with Him in the gospels. Walk with Him among the multitudes of desperate people clamoring for help and healing. Hear His tender response, feel His gentle touch. Go with Him to the lonely places to talk to the Father. Weep with Him in Gethsemane.

Know the power of His resurrection, the power of love. Be aware, though, that the love of Jesus is not from common stock— good feelings, warm fuzzies, sweet nothings. The power of Jesus' love is the selfless sort that, becoming vulnerable, volunteered to die, stormed the gates of hell on behalf of those He loved, and raised Himself to immortality so that His followers would know that they would follow suit.

Know His suffering. Bear your own heartache for Jesus willingly, humbly, and obediently in view of the glory that's coming in its wake.

Know His dying. He died a thousand times on the way to Calvary—to all of the inconveniences, the interruptions, the insults, the demands, and the misunderstandings. Practice those small deaths in your daily walk, so that when the real thing confronts you, you'll be ready.

Know His resurrection. Be fully alive to the kingdom of God in the here and now—understanding the hope of His calling as your vocation in life, trusting in the power of the Spirit as the source of your strength, and abiding in the presence of the Lord until He returns to take you home.

Love

Now that you have purified yourselves by obeying the truth
so that you have sincere love for your brothers, love one another deeply,
from the heart.

1 Peter 1:22

Love endures long and is patient and kind; love never is envious nor
boils over with jealousy, is not boastful or vainglorious, does not display
itself haughtily. It is not conceited (arrogant and inflated with pride);
it is not rude (unmannerly) and does not act unbecomingly.
Love (God's love in us) does not insist on its own rights or its own way,
for it is not self-seeking; it is not touchy or fretful or resentful; it takes
no account of the evil done to it [it pays no attention to a suffered
wrong]. It does not rejoice at injustice and unrighteousness,
but rejoices when right and truth prevail. Love bears up under anything
and everything that comes, is ever ready to believe the best of every
person, its hopes are fadeless under all circumstances, and it endures
everything [without weakening]. Love never fails [never fades out or
becomes obsolete or comes to an end].

1 Corinthians 13:4-8 AMP

This is how we know what real love is: Jesus gave his life for us.
So we should give our lives for our brothers and sisters.

1 John 3:16 NCV

Heavenly Father,

No matter how hard I try, I just can't seem to love some people. I've tried forgiving them, reaching out to them hoping the feeling would follow, confessing that I love them. But I know perfectly well that I'm deceiving myself and them—it's just an act, and that can't be pleasing to You.

I need Your help, Lord. Teach me to love as You love—from the heart. Point out to me the obstacles I've placed in the way of true, genuine love for these people. I'm sure there must be something that I'm not seeing because Your Word says that true love never fails (1 Corinthians 13:8). I open myself to You. Show me how to love in deed and in truth.

Amen.

AN IMPENETRABLE FORTRESS

When love is a decision that you make with your mind, it bends your will to a demonstration of virtues such as fairness, dependability, honesty, cooperation, and charity. In that temper of love, you treat people with a consideration respectful of the common thread of humanity that binds you together in the cosmos. It is a respectful, though distant, kind of love.

But when love is born of a determination within your heart, tender emissions of genuine concern spring from within your soul, reaching beyond the surface of shared origin and into the depths of the spirit. This love rests upon something more formidable than feelings; it is an impenetrable fortress built upon faith. It is an unrivaled commitment to those with whom you share the Lord. In other words, inspired by the love with which you have been loved, you love others.

Loving another deeply from the heart means more than well wishes. It means a proactive disposition which moves to relieve the heartaches of others, reaches to bear the burdens of others, and sacrifices to bring joy to others.

This love does not exasperate when neglected, nor does it make demands. It hurries to make amends for wrongs committed and does not hold those things in remembrance or recall them for the sake of retribution. It harbors no grudges, seeks no advantage, and finds no fault. It isn't jealous over time or attention because it is entirely forgetful of self.

It you want to love sincerely and from the heart, you'll have to dig deep, get honest, and give up the habit of loving yourself most.

My Precious Child,

You're right to think that love is something you can't fake. You know it isn't real, and the other person can see through your flimsy deception as well. It's time to face the fact that there are just some people you will never be able to love—on your own, that is. Even when you try to clothe yourself with love, sometimes you have to grow into the clothes. Still . . . you do have options.

When you find yourself in a situation in which your love—however well-intended—falls short of the mark, ask Me to love that person through you. Make yourself a channel for My strong, supernatural, eternal love to flow through you to the person in question. Do that long enough, and you will find your own ability to love deepened and purified.

Your loving Father

Motives

Search me, O God, and know my heart;
test me and know my thoughts.
Point out anything in me that offends you,
and lead me along the path of everlasting life.
Psalm 139:23-24 NLT

Acknowledge the God of your father, and serve him with wholehearted
devotion and with a willing mind, for the LORD searches every heart and
understands every motive behind the thoughts. If you seek him,
he will be found by you.
1 Chronicles 28:9

People may be pure in their own eyes,
but the LORD examines their motives.
Proverbs 16:2 NLT

Truly God is good to the upright,
to those who are pure in heart.
Psalm 73:1 RSV

Put me on trial, LORD, and cross-examine me.
Test my motives and affections.
Psalm 26:2 NLT

SOURED MILK

The issues over which you find yourself in conflict may betray the motives of your heart. Without warning, your loyalties, your prejudices, your passions, and your deepest ambitions are stripped naked in the heat of the battle. That isn't necessarily a negative thing. Remember how conflicted the Lord was when He encountered the thieving money-changers in the temple? He obviously wasn't concerned about being politically correct; He simply walked across the street to the leather smith, purchased a handful of cords, braided them into a respectable whip, and landed a smarting blow to the stinking philosophy that condones cheating a brother. (See John 2:14-15).

A struggle—whether private or public—that finds you doing battle for the sake of the oppressed or helpless may reveal a nobility of spirit that surprises even you.

On the other hand, conflict may peel away the protective layers of a corrupt heart, exposing dark, moldy patches of your character that you had hoped to keep concealed.

That was the case when a man of certain stature became incensed one day at the healing of a woman in bondage. "Indignant because Jesus had healed on the Sabbath, the synagogue ruler said to the people, 'There are six days for work. So come and be healed on those days, not on the Sabbath'" (Luke 13:14).

It wasn't simply the milk of human kindness that had soured within him; his courage had curdled as well. The coward hiding in his heart came rushing to the fore when, instead of confronting the Healer, he lashed out at the innocent spectators standing by. His true motives were exposed for all to see.

Obedience

If you are willing and obedient,
you will eat the best from the land.
Isaiah 1:19

What is more pleasing to the LORD: your burnt offerings and sacrifices
or your obedience to his voice? Obedience is far better than sacrifice.
Listening to him is much better than offering the fat of rams.
1 Samuel 15:22 NLT

Where there is no word from God, people are uncontrolled,
but those who obey what they have been taught are happy.
Proverbs 29:18 NCV

Those who obey what they are told will be rewarded.
Proverbs 13:13 NCV

When we obey him, every path he guides us on is fragrant
with his loving-kindness and his truth.
Psalm 25:10 TLB

Those who obey the commands protect themselves.
Proverbs 19:16 NCV

OBEDIENCE BAROMETER

Have you noticed that you submit readily to biblical directives that conform to your habits or values but are reticent and tend to rationalize when it comes to issues that challenge or inconvenience you?

A list of directives in Romans 12 may serve as an obedience barometer, revealing more about your willingness to obey God than you want to know:

· Despise and avoid evil in any form (media, humor).
· Cleave to goodness wherever you find it.
· Show devotion to others (without expecting anything in return).
· Treat others with selfless honor (respecting the disrespectful).
· Be fervent in spiritual matters, never compromising your zeal for the Lord.
· Serve the Lord (in specific capacities commensurate with your spiritual giftedness).
· Be joyful (when circumstances are trying).
· Be patient (in the midst of frustration).
· Be faithful (pray when you don't feel like it).
· Share with other believers (who need what you have).
· Be hospitable (though your house will get messy).
· Bless those who mistreat you (they will take advantage of you).
· Do not curse (even under your breath).
· Rejoice with people over their good fortune.
· Grieve with people over their losses.
· Live in such harmony with others that you become part of their symphony.
· Do not be proud (or stubborn).
· Fraternize with people who need you (not just people you need).
· Do not repay wound for wound.

Peace

When the ways of people please the LORD,
he causes even their enemies to be at peace with them.

Proverbs 16:7 NRSV

Jesus said, "I am leaving you with a gift—peace of mind and heart!
And the peace I give isn't fragile like the peace the world gives.
So don't be troubled or afraid."

John 14:27 TLB

Following after the Holy Spirit leads to life and peace.

Romans 8:6 TLB

Don't worry about anything; instead, pray about everything;
tell God your needs, and don't forget to thank him for his answers.
If you do this you will experience God's peace, which is far more
wonderful than the human mind can understand.
His peace will keep your thoughts and your hearts quiet
and at rest as you trust in Christ Jesus.

Philippians 4:6-7 TLB

Let the peace of heart that comes from Christ be always present
in your hearts and lives, for this is your responsibility and privilege as
members of his body. And always be thankful.

Colossians 3:15 TLB

Heavenly Father,

Half the time I don't know if I'm coming or going. So many decisions, responsibilities, obligations, activities, moral choices. I try to sort through them—usually late at night when I should be sleeping—but by morning, I'm caught up in the spin cycle again. I think maybe I need a lot of things, Lord, but mostly I need peace.

The angels who spoke to the shepherds at Your birth called You the Prince of Peace. And I need Your princely presence in my life in a big way. Come into my heart, Lord, and begin there. Show me where I have sacrificed peace for other things like power and vanity and prestige. Come into my chaos and clean house. And I'll give You all the glory for the results.

Amen.

WHAT YOU SEE IS WHO YOU ARE

When you live in conflict with your belief system, you are at war within yourself. Furthermore, when you contest the values of others, you have no peace with them either. In order to be at peace with yourself and the world around you, you must develop a deep sense of "being at one with yourself." That is a short way of saying, "Be the same person on the inside that you are on the outside," or "What you see is who you are."

A man named Sam experienced constant turmoil at work. He had a heavy-handed supervisor who expected Sam to agree with him on every issue. Sam did so, but at great cost—he sacrificed his peace of mind. He developed an ulcer and hypertension, not to mention a strained demeanor that affected his other relationships adversely. The more conflicted Sam became, the greater his lack of peace within and without became.

One day Sam came to the conclusion that he had taken all he could stand. Prepared to sacrifice his job, he walked into his supervisor's office and announced, "Sir, I have compromised my integrity in regard to my employment by going along with decisions that are inconsistent with my beliefs. I am prepared to give up my position, if need be, in order to rectify this dilemma. If not, you will detect a distinct change in my disposition from here forward."

"What will change in your disposition?" the supervisor asked.

"My convictions will no longer be disposable," Sam asserted.

Sam's boss reached out to shake his hand, saying, "Congratulations, Sam. I've been hoping your spine would show up!"

It takes courage to find peace.

My Precious Child,

It was for you that I brought peace to a chaotic world, and peace to your heart. It's been there—in you and all around you—since the day we met. The problem is that you can no longer feel it. You've become desensitized by a barrage of activities, advertising, well-meaning advice, and ethical compromise. You're tuned in to the wrong station.

Talk to Me in the morning before you start your day. That connects us—Spirit to spirit. Then as your day goes on, I can help you make choices, choose activities, set and maintain priorities, and purify your thoughts and motives. As these things begin to fall into place, the peace you desire will emerge in abundance.

Your loving Father

Perseverance

[Love] . . . always perseveres.

1 Corinthians 13:7

Blessed is the man who perseveres under trial, because when he has stood the test, he will receive the crown of life that God has promised to those who love him.

James 1:12

There are friends who pretend to be friends,
but there is a friend who sticks closer than a brother.

Proverbs 18:24 RSV

Pray in the Spirit at all times in every prayer and supplication. To that end keep alert and always persevere in supplication for all the saints.

Ephesians 6:18 NRSV

May the Lord direct your hearts into God's love and
Christ's perseverance.

2 Thessalonians 3:5

The testing of your faith develops perseverance. Perseverance must finish its work so that you may be mature and complete, not lacking anything.

James 1:3-4

TRUDGE THROUGH THE SLUDGE

Perseverance is one of the most demanding qualities you may develop. To persevere means to persist in a situation or in a relationship though you meet with resistance, opposition, discouragement, or any other counterinfluence. Persever-ance sounds noble from a philosophical perspective. But it is the nitty-gritty dirt and grime of real stick-to-itiveness, and it's difficult to pull off.

There are some prerequisites for learning perseverance in any endeavor or relationship. The first is that you must show up. You can't check out when things get tough, guarding yourself against all the messy clutter and chaos of people's hearts and then appearing again once order is restored. You must be willing to trudge through the sludge.

Second, be fully present. Don't be present in body, yet absent in spirit. There is nothing as discouraging as a plastic smile on a wooden face. You must focus on the situation—every part, good and bad—and respond appropriately—happy or sad.

Third, be prepared to get dirty, sweaty, stinky, and tired. You have not been appointed supervisor emeritus of the situation, standing aloof of the issue; you have been called into the trenches with the rest of humankind.

Fourth, don't chase the decoy. When called to persist in a difficult relationship, don't try to rationalize your way out by getting more deeply involved in another that is easier.

Finally, get over yourself. Be suspicious of your tendency to hypochondria, hypersensitivity, and hyperirritability associated with your preoccupation with your quota of "rest, privacy, and time away." If you are always missing opportunities to help others that involve manual labor, you may be avoiding your highest service.

Prayer

They'll pray to me by name
and I'll answer them personally.
I'll say, "That's my people."
They'll say, "GOD—my God!"
Zechariah 13:9 THE MESSAGE

Jesus said, "Here's what I want you to do: Find a quiet, secluded place so
you won't be tempted to role-play before God. Just be there as simply
and honestly as you can manage. The focus will shift from you to God,
and you will begin to sense his grace. The world is full of so-called
prayer warriors who are prayer-ignorant. They're full of formulas and
programs and advice, peddling techniques for getting what you want
from God. Don't fall for that nonsense. This is your Father you are
dealing with, and he knows better than you what you need. With a God
like this loving you, you can pray very simply."
Matthew 6:6-9 THE MESSAGE

Pray without ceasing.
1 Thessalonians 5:17 KJV

Why am I praying like this? Because I know you will answer me, O God!
Psalm 17:6 TLB

Heavenly Father,

How is it that You never tire of hearing from me?
It seems as if I'm constantly bringing You my problems and concerns, asking all kinds of questions, and
making a general nuisance of myself. Still . . . You
never brush me off or send me away. What do You see
in me and my feeble words?

Thank You, Lord, for always being there whenever
I need You—day or night. As soon as I start to talk, I
feel You near me. You are so faithful and loving. You
always make me feel welcome. You are always there to
listen and give me a new perspective on things. I look
forward to spending time with You.

Amen.

TALKING TO GOD

Because Jesus' mission was self-sacrificial, a great deal of inner strength was required in order for Him to take it up and carry it through to completion. That is probably why He spent so much time in prayer. He needed wisdom and guidance from His heavenly Father, and a complete outpouring of the Spirit so He could execute the high calling that was His alone.

Concerning prayer, the religious orientation of the day was radically different from Jesus' method. Prayer was regimented—done at certain times, by specific people, in particular places, and with precise phrases.

Jesus broke with the status quo, stirring up considerable controversy at this suggestion: "When you pray, go into your room, close the door and pray to your Father, who is unseen. Then your Father, who sees what is done in secret, will reward you" (Matthew 6:6). Insinuating that the common man could be rewarded by the Almighty without a religious formula, Jesus went so far as to suggest praying to God as "*Abba,*" suggesting intimacy with the Creator on the basis of sonship.

That is precisely the context in which Jesus prayed. He prayed spontaneously, like a son talking to his father; and intuitively, as if He really understood what was going on in the heart of God. He prayed in many places, at random times, with unconventional requests. His praying was personal and conversational. And most peculiar of all, Jesus prayed in such a way that there was dialogue between Himself and heaven.

No matter how you pray, God is listening, without judgment. He's always happy to hear from you. So relax and let prayer permeate your life—as Jesus did.

My Precious Child,

My Son, Jesus, died to reestablish a connection between us. Each time you come to Me in prayer, you honor His sacrifice. And I will never grow weary of hearing from you. After all, I love you very much.

Because you make time for Me, your life will be strewn with blessings straight from My throne. You will always be in a position to learn from Me. I will fill your mind with truth and wisdom. I will share mysteries with you. And as you grow in faith, I'll show you how to change your world. That line of communication between us is your lifeline and your greatest asset for living a powerful, purposeful life.

Your loving Father

Priorities

Jesus said, "Seek first the kingdom of God and His righteousness,
and all these things shall be added to you."
Matthew 6:33 NKJV

Remember to observe the Sabbath as a holy day. Six days a week are
for your daily duties and your regular work, but the seventh day is a day
of Sabbath rest before the Lord your God. On that day you
are to do no work of any kind.
Exodus 20:8-10 TLB

Those who wait on the LORD will find new strength.
They will fly high on wings like eagles. They will run and not grow weary.
They will walk and not faint.
Isaiah 40:31 NLT

It is senseless for you to work so hard from early morning until
late at night, fearing you will starve to death;
for God wants his loved ones to get their proper rest.
Psalm 127:2 TLB

You chart the path ahead of me and tell me where to stop and rest.
Every moment you know where I am.
Psalm 139:3 TLB

THE PRIORITY PUZZLE

If you're like most people, you've discovered that setting priorities is tricky business. Even if you go about it in an orderly manner—realistically assessing the hours in your day, subtracting those hours that are nonnegotiable, and ordering the remainder according to urgency and importance—you could still have water flooding through the dike at an alarming rate.

Our all-knowing God anticipated that we would have trouble putting first things first. That's why He instructed us to set aside a day every week—a day to step away from the hurry and demands of the world—to renew and refresh ourselves.

Giving up Sunday as an extra day to get things done may seem like a great way to make your situation worse instead of better. But like many of God's principles, the opposite is probably true. Making rest a priority could leave you with more energy to tend to other priorities. Giving yourself time to think, time to pray, time to reflect on God's goodness pays off in terms of clearheaded efficiency, better choices, creative solutions, and a positive attitude.

Now this doesn't just mean attending church. It also means resting your mind and body, giving yourself a break, putting the busyness on hold. And you may not choose Sunday as your Lord's Day. That's up to you.

Let God help you keep your priorities in place by putting rest, relationship, and spiritual refreshment in their proper place. You will have to step out in faith before you see results, but once you do, you're sure to find things falling into place for the rest of the week.

Purity

Jesus said,
"Blessed are the pure in heart,
for they will see God."
Matthew 5:8

Who may ascend into the hill of the LORD?
Or who may stand in His holy place?
He who has clean hands and a pure heart.
Psalm 24:3-4 NKJV

Even a child is known by his deeds,
Whether what he does is pure and right.
Proverbs 20:11 NKJV

God, examine me and know my heart; . . .
See if there is any bad thing in me.
Lead me on the road to everlasting life.
Psalm 139:23-24 NCV

Happy are those who live pure lives,
who follow the LORD'S teachings.
Psalm 119:1 NCV

PURE AND SIMPLE

Many people think of words like *chastity* and *virtue* when considering the concept of purity, and they are correct. But when Jesus told His followers that unless they changed their ways and became as little children they would not inherit the kingdom of God, the quality about which He spoke was likely purity of heart—meaning that their motives, thoughts, words, actions, and reactions should be true, honest, and unadulterated. The kind of purity He was addressing in that statement stems from authenticity. Children are so genuine, so real, so pure in heart. They bear a greater resemblance to the heavenly Father because they haven't yet been polluted by the deceit of the world. With children, what you see is what you get—pure and simple.

Suppose your father, a wealthy oil tycoon, just died. If you are normal, you probably hope for a respectable inheritance upon disclosure of the will. But what if your mother had fallen from your father's good graces years back, your siblings didn't recognize you anymore, and your birth certificate had been destroyed in a fire at county hall twenty years earlier? How would you prove your eligibility to receive your inheritance? You would likely seek scientific proof of the purity of your descent: DNA testing.

Fortunately, your heavenly Father will never die; yet when it comes to your inheritance in the kingdom of God, the only proof of eligibility is still the purity of your descent—meaning, the imprint of your heavenly Father on your heart.

Purpose

Jesus said, "When you give a feast, invite the poor, the maimed, the lame, the blind. And you will be blessed, because they cannot repay you; for you shall be repaid at the resurrection of the just."

Luke 14:13-14 NKJV

Jesus said, "People who are well don't need a doctor! It's the sick people who do! . . . Now go away and learn the meaning of this verse of Scripture, 'It isn't your sacrifices and your gifts I want —I want you to be merciful.' For I have come to urge sinners, not the self-righteous, back to God."

Matthew 9:12-13 TLB

If a man comes into your church dressed in expensive clothes and with valuable gold rings on his fingers, and at the same moment another man comes in who is poor and dressed in threadbare clothes, and you make a lot of fuss over the rich man and give him the best seat in the house and say to the poor man, "You can stand over there if you like, or else sit on the floor"—well, judging a man by his wealth shows that you are guided by wrong motives.

James 2:2-4 TLB

ALWAYS HUG THE FAT KID

Having hired the young man as a guide two weeks earlier, Jim wondered whether he had made the right decision.

"Son, this is a mountain trek for people who are seeking a spiritual adventure," he announced to Matt one afternoon. "You can't go picking up hitchhikers from the side of the road and bringing them to base camp."

"I thought our purpose was to help people," Matt countered, dangling a toothpick from the side of his mouth.

"We are—but only those who are registered."

"Oh, I see." Matt scratched his chin, looking pensive. "You mean to say, only paying customers can benefit from our services."

"Of course that's not what I mean." Jim felt exasperation rising in his chest.

"What do you mean, then?" Matt's gaze locked onto Jim.

"It's just that I'm responsible for the experience and enjoyment that these fine folks have purchased, and I can't have vagabonds coming into the camp."

"What can it hurt if some less fortunate people join us around the campfire before we ascend to the heights?" Matt pressed.

"It isn't what this journey represents." Jim was struggling to convey his line of reasoning. "It's kind of like having some fat kid barge into a fitness spa. The patrons of good health and physical fitness can't embrace him. It's disruptive and inconsistent with their orientation, that's all."

"Gotcha!" Matt flicked the toothpick into the woods and turned to walk away.

The next night, it was Matt's turn to deliver the thoughts around the campfire.

"My fellow trekkers," he began, standing with his hands clasped calmly behind his back, "no matter what . . . always hug the fat kid."

Quietness and Solitude

Very early in the morning, while it was still dark, Jesus got up,
left the house and went off to a solitary place, where he prayed.

Mark 1:35

God says, "Be quiet and know that I am God."

Psalm 46:10 NCV

Because the Lord is my Shepherd, I have everything I need!
He lets me rest in the meadow grass and leads me
beside the quiet streams.

Psalm 23:1-2 TLB

I have stilled and quieted my soul;
like a weaned child with its mother,
like a weaned child is my soul within me.

Psalm 131:2

I wait quietly before God,
for my salvation comes from him.

Psalm 62:1 NLT

COME EARLY AND COME ALONE

Moses had been the Lord's right-hand man. Through the conflict with Pharaoh over the release of the Israelites, through the months of the miraculous plagues, through the Passover and deliverance of Israel from Egyptian bondage, through the passage between the walls of water at the Red Sea, and now through the wilderness to Sinai, he served God faithfully.

Moses was accustomed to having discourse with the Lord on a daily basis during the period of the Exodus. It would seem to any observer that Moses was in an intimate relationship with the Almighty. However, he hungered for more.

After the Lord inscribed the Ten Commandments and Moses returned to camp to find the Israelites engaged in an idolatrous worship, Moses cried out to the Lord for a deeper disclosure. He longed to commune with his God in ways he could not relate to man.

"You have said, 'I know you by name and you have found favor with Me. . . .' Now show me Your glory." (See Exodus 33:17-18.)

God agreed to honor Moses' bold request. He said, "Be ready in the morning, and then come up on Mount Sinai. Present yourself to Me there on top of the mountain. No one is to come with you." (See Exodus 34:2-3.)

The two stipulations the Lord put on His self-disclosure were that Moses come in the quiet of the early morning, and that he come alone.

In a world like ours, you've got to get up early in order to hear the silence. The quiet morning hours are the only time of the day when you can be relatively sure that you can commune with God uninterrupted. Some things—like solitude— never change.

Redemption

You know that it was not with perishable things such as silver or gold that
you were redeemed from the empty way of life handed down to you
from your forefathers, but with the precious blood of Christ.

1 Peter 1:18-19

When someone becomes a Christian, he becomes a
brand new person inside. He is not the same anymore.
A new life has begun! All these new things are from God
who brought us back to himself through what Christ Jesus did.

2 Corinthians 5:17-18 TLB

With the LORD there is mercy,
And with Him is abundant redemption.

Psalm 130:7 NKJV

In Him we have redemption through His blood, the forgiveness of sins,
according to the riches of His grace.

Ephesians 1:7 NKJV

He has delivered us from the power of darkness and conveyed us into
the kingdom of the Son of His love, in whom we have redemption
through His blood, the forgiveness of sins.

Colossians 1:13-14 NKJV

Heavenly Father,

I can't imagine where I would be if You had not redeemed my life, paid the price to change my course, and given me a second chance. I made such a terrible mess of things on my own. Somehow You looked past my failures and ridiculously poor choices, past my arrogance, past all my issues and hang-ups. Don't ask me how, but You saw something worth saving in me.

I may never understand why You love me, but I'm glad You do. You've brought hope back into my life. My loneliness is gone. You've stilled the storm that was constantly raging in my mind. You've even given me a song of joy to sing. Me—joy! That's a miracle for sure. Thank You, Lord, for the power of Your redemptive love.

Amen.

FREE TO WALK AWAY

What did you bring with you into adulthood from your family of origin that you wish you had left behind? Your father's temper? Your grandmother's critical spirit? Your mom's depression? Haunting memories of neglect or abuse? A tarnished reputation? A lack of integrity? Fear? Worry? Laziness?

You—like everyone else—have some unwanted baggage or undesirable traits that you would happily discard if only you could.

Here's the good news: You can!

Jesus bought you back from those negative things handed to you from your family of origin, your cultural surroundings, and your environmental orientation. You are free to walk away from them. Your past, present, and future have been redeemed—bought and paid for—by the One who is able to make all things new.

How do you take hold of a truth such as that? How do you make it real?

The answer is, you take hold of Jesus. Whatever your unwanted baggage is, begin by going to Jesus and laying it at His feet in prayer. "Here I am, Lord, where I belong. Fear [anger, heartache, depression] doesn't possess me anymore. Your blood has paid my way to freedom; so I appeal to the blood. Open my heart and mind to embrace this newfound freedom."

You'll find that little by little, day by day, the thing you wish to leave behind will begin to lose its grip upon your heart. That's the power of redemption.

My Precious Child,

I created you—how could I help but love you? And even when you turned away from Me, even when you sold yourself to a cruel master, I continued to love you and want you back. The cost of your redemption was high—the highest price ever paid. It was the precious blood of My Son, Jesus, who was willing to give His life as a sacrifice for your rebellion and unfaithfulness.

Do not take this second chance for granted. Cling to it, and it will continue to change your life and give you hope and purpose. Whenever you have an opportunity, tell others about what has happened to you. It will serve to remind you of your incalculable worth to Me, while making others aware that their lives can be redeemed as well.

Your loving Father

Rejection

Jesus said, "I am the bread of life. No one who comes to me will ever be hungry again. . . . Those the Father has given me will come to me, and I will never reject them."

John 6:35,37 NLT

The LORD who created you says: "Do not be afraid, for I have ransomed you. I have called you by name; you are mine."

Isaiah 43:1 NLT

I have put my words in your mouth and hidden you safe within my hand. I planted the stars in place and molded all the earth. I am the one who says to Israel, "You are mine."

Isaiah 51:16 TLB

Jesus said, "The one who rejects you, rejects me. And rejecting me is the same as rejecting God, who sent me."

Luke 10:16 THE MESSAGE

Jesus said, "If anyone hears what I am saying and doesn't take it seriously, I don't reject him. I didn't come to reject the world; I came to save the world."

John 12:47-48 THE MESSAGE

HAVE MERCY ON ME

Just outside of Jericho, where the road was teeming with travelers, blind Bartimaeus sat begging. He could hear the steady shuffling of feet and the cheerful banter between sighted men.

Suddenly, he heard another sound, the faint roar of a crowd. At first, Bartimaeus feared it would be another fruitless day of begging.

But wait! This was different—the din of a multitude. Yet why was a multitude coming to Jericho?

Hearing the labored breath of a young man approaching, Bartimaeus swiped at the air to grasp hold of him as he passed. "What's going on?" he demanded.

Pulling his arm free, the boy answered, "Jesus of Nazareth is passing through here."

Bartimaeus's darkened eyes widened. "Jesus!" he shouted. He began running toward the sound of the crowd, waving his arms above his head, "Jesus! Son of David!"

The youth ran after him, "Shhh!" he commanded. "Don't interrupt the Teacher."

"Jesus! Son of David! Have mercy!"

Jesus slowed His step, craning His neck to search the crowd. Someone had appealed to the King.

Another man moved to quiet him. "Be quiet!" he warned. "You have no right to interrupt . . ."

The familiar dagger of rejection penetrated the blind man's heart. He had felt it many times in his life, but he had heard that this Rabbi was different.

"Jesus!" he screamed. "Son of David! Have mercy."

Just then the voice of another sounded in his keen ears: "Bring him here to Me." (See Mark 10:45-52.)

In the presence of Jesus, there is no such thing as rejection.

Relationships

You are not the same as those who do not believe.
So do not join yourselves to them. Good and bad do not
belong together. Light and darkness cannot share together.
2 Corinthians 6:14 NCV

As iron sharpens iron,
so people can improve each other.
Proverbs 27:17 NCV

He who walks with the wise grows wise,
but a companion of fools suffers harm.
Proverbs 13:20

Do not make friends with a hot-tempered man,
do not associate with one easily angered,
or you may learn his ways
and get yourself ensnared.
Proverbs 22:24-25

Can two walk together, except they be agreed?
Amos 3:3 KJV

FOR WHAT PURPOSE?

What difference would it make if you knew the specific purpose for each of your relationships? Some of them are easy to assess: Spousal relationships, for instance, have obvious implications. But what about friendships, professional relationships, spiritual intimates, and acquaintances?

In the Scriptures, you see examples of relationships that served a purpose greater than self-fulfillment; they served the kingdom. Some of them were short-lived, and others were life-long commitments. Some had a far-reaching impact, and some were narrower in scope. Isn't it possible that the same is true in your life? If you knew the purpose each of your relationships could serve, you might be a better steward of your relational resources, investing in those that will mean glory to God.

On a piece of paper, write in one column the ten relationships (other than family) upon which you expend the majority of your time, energy, emotions, and effort—both negative and positive. You will find that they aren't all close friends—some might even be enemies.

Now write in the other column the fruit of the Spirit: love, joy, peace, patience, kindness, goodness, faithfulness, gentleness, and self-control.

If you evaluate each name on your list in light of each of the characteristics of the Spirit, you'll arrive at some interesting conclusions. Some of your relationships are an investment in your well-being, extending the fruit of the Spirit in your direction. Other relationships require that you grow in your spiritual character. And there may be others that are a downward drag to your personal well-being and should be pruned off.

Relationships—whether negative or positive—should ultimately serve to glorify God. Those that don't may not be essential.

Renewal

Hide your face from my sins
and blot out all my iniquity.
Create in me a pure heart, O God,
and renew a steadfast spirit within me.

Psalm 51:9-10

Those who wait for the LORD shall renew their strength,
they shall mount up with wings like eagles,
they shall run and not be weary,
they shall walk and not faint.

Isaiah 40:31 NRSV

The LORD satisfies your desires with good things
so that your youth is renewed like the eagle's.

Psalm 103:5

We do not lose heart. Though our outer nature is wasting away,
our inner nature is being renewed every day.

2 Corinthians 4:16 RSV

Heavenly Father,

I've always been one of those people with an end-less supply of energy. I can accomplish more in a day than most people can do in a week. But lately, something inside me has changed. I've lost my drive, my fervor. Life seems to have lost its color and excitement. I wonder if it all means anything at all.

I don't like myself this way, Lord, but I don't know how to regain my enthusiasm for life, and I can't even get excited about looking for it. I'm too proud to let anyone down, so I go through the motions, but my heart isn't in it. You're the only One who can help me, Lord. I need Your strong, encouraging hand to get me up and running again.

Amen.

MAGS, MEDS, AND MUG SHOTS

The subscription to your favorite magazine expires, so you mail in a renewal. The prescription for your allergy medication expires, so you pay a visit to your physician, drop by the drugstore on the corner, and renew it. Your driver's license expires, so you make the dreaded trek to the DMV, sit for two-and-a-half hours, smile for a new mug shot, and renew it. So . . . what do you do when your passion for the Lord expires?

There comes a time in every life for spiritual renewal; in fact, several. The question is, does there exist a prescribed formula for how to effectively accomplish it; one that has a guarantee with a specific deadline for expiration, like your mags, your meds, and your mug shot?

Unfortunately, that isn't the way relationships work—and that is precisely what you are dealing with, a relationship. Unlike these other things, your spiritual well-being is not a function of forms, examinations, or snapshots. It is simply a matter of the heart. And just like any relationship, it suffers a great deal from neglect or abuse.

So what should you do in the case of a heart grown cold? Do what your common sense tells you about relationships: go to God, confess your wayward heart, confide in Him how this came to pass, ask Him to forgive you and help you, and then rejoice in the renewal. There is no penance to be paid. There is nothing to earn back. There is only the free gift of His amazing grace.

The good news is that He is always waiting to receive you, for He makes all things new!

My Precious Child,

You are a wonderful, gifted person, and I've watched with delight as you have used your gifts to serve others. But it seems that your great natural abilities have caused you to depend too much on yourself for strength and motivation and too little on Me. In the process, you've burned out, spent yourself. Your motives were noble, but that does not change the outcome.

There is a way back to where you were, but it will mean a change in emphasis. You must learn to let Me set the pace, provide the motivation, uplift, and strengthen you. That won't always be easy because your natural inclination is to run rather than to walk, to initiate rather than to follow. But if you will trust Me and listen carefully for My voice, I promise to renew you mentally, emotionally, and spiritually.

Your loving Father

Repentance

If we say that we have fellowship with Him, and walk in darkness,
we lie and do not practice the truth. But if we walk in the light as He
is in the light, we have fellowship with one another, and the blood of
Jesus Christ His Son cleanses us from all sin.

1 John 1:6-7 NKJV

Don't you realize how patient he is being with you? . . .
Can't you see that he has been waiting all this time without
punishing you, to give you time to turn from your sin?
His kindness is meant to lead you to repentance.

Romans 2:4 TLB

Against You, You only, have I sinned,
And done this evil in Your sight . . .
Purge me with hyssop, and I shall be clean;
Wash me, and I shall be whiter than snow.

Psalm 51:4, 7 NKJV

Repent! Turn away from all your offenses; then sin will not be your
downfall. Rid yourselves of all the offenses you have committed,
and get a new heart and a new spirit.

Ezekiel 18:30-31

A PURPOSE BEYOND FORGIVENESS

The need for repentance is constant. Since there is no one who does not sin, it follows that there is no one who does not need to repent. In our culture, however, repentance has been buried in long-forgotten archives of religion because sin has been so effectively renamed. What constituted a trespass in Jesus' day now appears to be a vast catalog of psychological disorders and addictive behaviors. When convinced that you are dealing not with sin, but with a psychosis or a behavioral dilemma instead, it is therapy—not repentance—that seems to be in order. Unfortunately, we have lost something good in the process.

Repentance serves purposes beyond forgiveness. It puts your heart into the humble posture of receiving and realigns your mortal soul with proper regard for the Sovereign of the universe. It helps you to admit your dependency upon the only One able to rescue you, and it goes a long way toward refining your character and strengthening your integrity.

The new remedies may work on a humanistic level—men and women reaching within themselves for a change of thought and behavior. But they fall short, neglecting the spiritual. Only repentance can reestablish your relationship with God and get you back on the path of total wellness—body, soul, and spirit. Only repentance can realign you with God's powerful plan for your life. Only repentance adds the power of the Holy Spirit to your list of resources as you fight to remain free of sin.

In truth, it need not be one or the other—both repentance and therapy bring something to the table, as long as you remember that therapies often fail, but God never does.

Restoration

Restore us, O God;
make your face shine upon us,
that we may be saved.

Psalm 80:3

The LORD says:
"If you repent, I will restore you
that you may serve me."

Jeremiah 15:19

The LORD restores my soul.
He leads me in paths of righteousness
for his name's sake.

Psalm 23:3 RSV

Remember that you were at that time separated from Christ . . . having
no hope and without God in the world. But now in Christ Jesus you
who once were far off have been brought near in the blood of Christ.
For he is our peace, who has made us both one, and has broken down
the dividing wall of hostility.

Ephesians 2:12-14 RSV

As far as the east is from the west,
so far he removes our transgressions from us.
As a father has compassion for his children,
so the LORD has compassion for those who fear him.
For he knows how we were made;
he remembers that we are dust.

Psalm 103:12-14 NRSV

DO YOU LOVE ME?

After the events of the Crucifixion and Resurrection, a handful of disciples are fishing. Peter is among them. Though elated that the Lord is alive, he is struggling with depression. Peter has discovered his own weakness, his unfaithfulness . . . the truth about the man he is when under pressure.

A stranger stands on the shore. "Have you any fish?"

"No," they answer.

"Try the other side of the boat; there's a whale of a catch there."

No sooner do they cast over, but the net is full of fish. John looks at Peter and grins, "It's got to be the Lord!"

Unable to restrain his impulse, Peter dives in and swims to shore.

"Simon, son of John," Jesus addresses Peter, looking him in the eye. That was Peter's old identity—the name he had before he received the call to discipleship. It hurts him to hear the Lord say it now, after he failed the test of true discipleship.

"Simon, son of John," He says again. "Do you love Me?"

Surely, Jesus doesn't mean to wound him . . . or does He, since Peter had wounded Him so deeply?

Then for the third time, "Simon, son of John, do you love Me?"

Peter's heart is broken. *Since I denied the Lord when He needed me most, He's obviously turning me out.*

"Follow Me!" Jesus concluded.

What? He reinstated the call?

Though it was a genuine setback, Jesus had known the truth about Peter's weakness from the beginning. Having never lost sight of Peter's human condition, the call still stood. Restoration is a brand-new start in the human heart—a fresh call from the Friend most faithful. (See John 21:5-7.)

Resurrection

Jesus said, "I am the resurrection and the life.
Those who believe in me will have life even if they die.
And everyone who lives and believes in me will never die."

John 11:25-26 NCV

We were buried with Him through baptism into death,
that just as Christ was raised from the dead by the glory of the Father,
even so we also should walk in newness of life. For if we have been united
together in the likeness of His death, certainly we also shall be
in the likeness of His resurrection.

Romans 6:4-5 NKJV

Praise be to the God and Father of our Lord Jesus Christ!
In his great mercy he has given us new birth into a living hope through
the resurrection of Jesus Christ from the dead, and into an inheritance
that can never perish, spoil or fade—kept in heaven for you.

1 Peter 1:3-4

If the Spirit of Him who raised Jesus from the dead dwells in you,
He who raised Christ from the dead will also give life to your mortal
bodies through His Spirit who dwells in you.

Romans 8:11 NKJV

PASSAGE THROUGH DEATH

The wonder of the Resurrection holds greater significance for the human soul than initially meets the eye. It appears that a crucified Messiah arose simply as the glorified King. In fact, He did! But that isn't all that the Resurrection intended to witness to you. It is only the beginning.

The Resurrection of Jesus publishes a new world order—a new humanity fit for a new existence. Jesus' actual body was raised from the grave, but it was a glorified version of the old DNA. He was put into that tomb in a mortal body; He was raised an immortal soul. Something happened in that passage through death that has direct implications for you.

Here are four of those implications. Take them personally:

1. He became The Walker-through-the-Walls: Before the Resurrection, Jesus voluntarily subjected Himself to the physical laws of nature much like any other mortal. But after that Sunday, His physical being became subject to His spiritual pre-eminence. He can penetrate the most formidable barrier, including your stubborn heart.

2. He empowered His followers for mission: Just after the Resurrection, Jesus breathed on His disciples and said, "Receive the Holy Spirit." As His follower, you have been anointed and commissioned by Jesus to carry on the work that He began.

3. He passed through the atmosphere without incinerating: The transforming power of the Resurrection is the only means by which you will get off this planet alive. The new, immortal version of your old earthy self will be equipped to withstand the elements and be lifted into the highest heavens.

4. He was welcomed home by His Father, and one day, you will be welcomed home as well.

Rewards

The Lord himself is my inheritance, my prize.
He is my food and drink, my highest joy!
Psalm 16:5 TLB

In a race everyone runs, but only one person gets first prize.
So run your race to win. To win the contest you must deny yourselves
many things that would keep you from doing your best. An athlete goes
to all this trouble just to win a blue ribbon or a silver cup, but we do it
for a heavenly reward that never disappears.
1 Corinthians 9:24-25 TLB

The LORD rewarded me for doing right;
he compensated me because of my innocence.
Psalm 18:20 NLT

The laws of the LORD are true; each one is fair.
… There is great reward for those who obey them.
Psalm 19:9,11 NLT

Day by day the LORD takes care of the innocent,
and they will receive a reward that lasts forever.
Psalm 37:18 NLT

THE FRIEND OF GOD

Church people are always talking about eternal rewards. What kind of rewards would you find appealing?

Heaven? If you are like most people, you think of heaven as a place of ethereal splendor. You picture the throne of God and the angels gathering round with their harps, singing. You might imagine streets paved with precious gold, halls of shimmering white marble, and gates of pearl. Perhaps you envision a mansion there, with a great banquet table and an unending supply of the finest foods.

Or how about eternal life? To some, it is the matter of immortality that holds forth the greatest promise. Never having to face disease or death. The security of a peaceful existence in a paradise of the soul.

Maybe it's rescue from the alternative—eternity without God's loving presence. Some people are highly motivated by what they don't want.

But Jesus said the true glory of eternal reward is intimacy with the Almighty—that you may know Him and be known by Him. Here, and in the hereafter, you are to experience the inconceivable privilege of mutual disclosure with the Creator and Sustainer of the universe. God has made Himself knowable through the visual aid He sent in His Son. And He longs to be with you in Spirit so that you can become one heart and one mind with Him.

The place, the terms, the security . . . these are all wonderful aspects of your eternal reward. But being the friend of God . . . now that will be glory!

Righteousness

Righteousness from God comes through faith in Jesus Christ
to all who believe. There is no difference, for all have sinned and
fall short of the glory of God, and are justified freely by his grace through
the redemption that came by Christ Jesus.

Romans 3:22-24

The kingdom of God is not a matter of eating and drinking,
but of righteousness, peace and joy in the Holy Spirit, because anyone
who serves Christ in this way is pleasing to God.

Romans 14:17-18

God made him who had no sin to be sin for us,
so that in him we might become the righteousness of God.

2 Corinthians 5:21

This Good News tells us that God makes us ready for heaven—makes us
right in God's sight—when we put our faith and trust in Christ to save
us. This is accomplished from start to finish by faith.

Romans 1:17 TLB

A PARABLE RETOLD

"To some who were confident of their own righteousness and looked down on everybody else, Jesus told this parable." (See Luke 18:9-14.)

Two women went to church one day. One had been the wife of a deacon for thirty-one years and the mother of four children—all with college degrees from Christian universities. She never missed a prayer meeting, never touched alcohol or tobacco or engaged in illicit sex, and always attended the Ladies' Bible Class on Tuesdays. She maintained a pristine reputation within the community.

The other woman was divorced, pregnant, and had a drinking problem.

The first woman stood up and prayed about herself: "Lord, I thank You that I am not like other women—partying, sleeping around, and bringing shame upon the Church—or even like that woman on the back pew who failed in her marriage, is drunk half the time, and doesn't even know whose baby she is carrying. I read my Bible every day, pray every night, and never watch an R-rated movie."

Meanwhile, the brokenhearted woman in the back of the building collapsed onto the floor in a heap, crying. She couldn't even lift her head, but dropped it heavily into her hands and sobbed, "God, have mercy on me. I'm such a sinner."

I tell you that this one, rather than the first, went home justified before God. For everyone who exalts himself will be humbled, and he who humbles himself will be exalted.

Sacrifice

Put your trust in the Lord, and offer him pleasing sacrifices.

Psalm 4:5 TLB

Brothers and sisters, since God has shown us great mercy,
I beg you to offer your lives as a living sacrifice to him.

Romans 12:1 NCV

I will not sacrifice to the LORD my God burnt offerings
that cost me nothing.

2 Samuel 24:24

May he remember all your offerings
and accept all your sacrifices.

Psalm 20:3 NCV

The sacrifice God wants is a broken spirit.
God, you will not reject a heart that is broken and sorry for sin.

Psalm 51:17 NCV

We know love by this, that he laid down his life for us
—and we ought to lay down our lives for one another.
How does God's love abide in anyone who has the world's goods
and sees a brother or sister in need and yet refuses help?

1 John 3:16-17 NRSV

Heavenly Father,

I can never repay You for all the sacrifices You've made for me. All I can do is bring to You all that I have—and I gladly give it, every part of it, to the One who has invested so much in me.

Lord, I give You my time. I promise to be there each day, waiting in Your presence. Hold me as long as You like, or send me on my way. It is no sacrifice to spend time with You. I give You my love, all of it. It is no sacrifice to empty my heart at Your feet. I give You my future, without reservation. It is no sacrifice to give the promise of what I might become to the One who gave me life in the first place. I give You my all. It is no sacrifice to lose myself in You, my Savior and my God.

Amen.

WHERE DOES GOD FIGURE IN?

We all make sacrifices—but most often our generosity is limited to those things we really hold dear. Can you name who, or what, it is in your life? It might be easier if you think of it in terms of time, money, comfort, or energy.

To what/whom is your time allotted? Is it your career? Your appearance? How about recreation? Could it be entertainment, gossip, or travel? Maybe it is your children, your spouse, or even your mother. It might be your house, your vehicle, your computer, or even your dog. Don't be deceived—it could be hiking, reading, or daydreaming.

What about your financial resources? There is no truer indicator of your priorities than your pocketbook. Where does your money go? Groceries and the mortgage? How about to the shopping mall and salon? Perhaps it goes to golf or gambling. Maybe airline tickets and expensive restaurants. It could be that you just hoard the majority of it for yourself.

What about your energy? Who or what gets the best hours of your day, the most enthusiastic part of you, and the greatest investment of your vibrant personality?

The honest answers to those penetrating questions will tell you for whom or what you are willing to sacrifice.

So ask yourself: Did God figure in there anywhere? It cost the Almighty Abba the life of His only Son . . . whom He loved. You were the one for whom He made the sacrifice. How much would you sacrifice for Him?

My Precious Child,

Though you may think your sacrifices are small and unimpressive, in My eyes they are precious beyond measure. And I give you My word, nothing you give to Me will ever be wasted. Instead, I will mold and shape your offering and return it to you, radiating with life and vitality, a blessing to all those whose lives you touch.

As you give your time to Me, you will find that you have more time, not less—time to reap the bounty of life. As you give Me your love, you will find your heart overflowing with love from a heavenly source. As you give Me your future, you will find open doors and exciting opportunities coming your way in abundance. Whatever you give to Me, whatever the nature of your sacrifice, will be greatly multiplied to you again.

Your loving Father

Seeking God

Glory in his holy name;
Let all rejoice who seek the Lord.
Seek the Lord; yes, seek his strength
And seek his face untiringly.

1 Chronicles 16:10-11 TLB

All who seek the Lord shall find him and shall praise his name.
Their hearts shall rejoice with everlasting joy. The whole earth shall see
it and return to the Lord.

Psalm 22:26-27 TLB

The LORD looked down from heaven on all people
to see … if anyone was looking to God for help.

Psalm 14:2 NCV

Those who know your name put their trust in you;
for you, O LORD, have not forsaken those who seek you.

Psalm 9:10 NRSV

The LORD looks down from heaven on humankind
to see if there are any who are wise,
who seek after God.

Psalm 14:2 NRSV

STRANGER ON THE CORNER

"In the thirty-ninth year of his reign Asa was afflicted with a disease in his feet. Though his disease was severe, even in his illness he did not seek help from the LORD, but only from the physicians" (2 Chronicles 16:12). Within two years, he was dead.

"What's wrong with seeking the help of physicians?" you ask. Absolutely nothing. The point is Asa sought help only from the physicians. It is an insult to the Almighty when His people pursue every avenue of assistance, guidance, comfort, and support other than Himself.

Suppose a stranger is standing at the corner of the street watching as a little boy learns to ride the bike his father just bought him. The father runs behind the bike time after time, holding to the back of the seat so the boy doesn't fall. He coaches and encourages his son throughout the morning, building his confidence.

Finally, the boy yells, "Let go, Dad! I think I can do it."

The father hesitantly releases his grip, though his heart is hanging on a thread.

The handlebar wobbles slightly, and the boy suddenly loses his balance and falls, scraping his knee and bruising his ego.

The father runs to his side, reaching with loving arms to help him, but the little guy pushes his hands away—dodging his concern—and runs into the arms of the stranger on the corner, crying to him for help.

Wouldn't happen, you say. Probably not. But it does happen with our heavenly Father. He loves you and has given you everything you have. Don't turn to a stranger for help. Place yourself and your problems right into His waiting arms.

Service

Serve the LORD with gladness!
Come into his presence with singing!
Psalm 100:2 RSV

Get to know the God of your ancestors. Worship and serve him with
your whole heart and with a willing mind. For the LORD sees every heart
and understands and knows every plan and thought.
1 Chronicles 28:9 NLT

Jesus said, "Your attitude must be like my own, for I, the Messiah,
did not come to be served, but to serve, and to give my life
as a ransom for many."
Matthew 20:28 TLB

Jesus said, "The one who serves you best will be your leader.
Out in the world the master sits at the table and is served by his servants.
But not here! For I am your servant."
Luke 22:26-27 TLB

Never be lazy in your work, but serve the Lord enthusiastically.
Romans 12:11 TLB

THE FARMER WHO WAGED WAR

Gideon was a humble farmer in Israel when God called him to greatness. While secretly threshing wheat at a wine-press in order to conceal it from an enemy, the astonished young man was confronted by the angel of the Lord, who said, "The Lord is with you, mighty warrior" (Judges 6:12).

He was probably a bit taken back by that greeting simply because—Gideon was not a mighty warrior! He was a regular guy just trying to survive in the midst of a great oppression. But Gideon discovered, in time, that the Lord's greeting was prophetic. He was speaking of Gideon's potential. He alone knew what He had equipped Gideon to do, and He had come to call on His investment and put Gideon into service on behalf of God's people.

The mission was prepared and assigned far in advance of Gideon's calling; and the calling itself was commensurate with the gifts and abilities with which the Lord had empowered him.

Sure enough, after several clarifying discussions with the Almighty, Gideon—with a mere three hundred men—stood up to a fearsome foe, blowing horns, breaking jars, and shouting, "A sword for the Lord and for Gideon!" (Judges 7:20). The unconventional commotion of Gideon's radical faith put the enemy to flight.

You—like Gideon—have been called into service. You don't see yourself as a great servant, but the Lord knows your potential. Perhaps, like Gideon, you need to stand up in the face of the enemies that are harassing your life and the lives of those you know and make a commotion. Champion God's kingdom, rescue the perishing . . . serve the Lord!

Sincerity

Now that you have purified yourselves by obeying the truth so
that you have sincere love for your brothers, love one another deeply,
from the heart. . . . Rid yourselves of all malice and all deceit,
hypocrisy, envy, and slander of every kind.

1 Peter 1:22; 2:1

In everything we have done in the world, and especially with you,
we have had an honest and sincere heart from God. We did this by
God's grace, not by the kind of wisdom the world has.

2 Corinthians 1:12 NCV

Obey your earthly masters with respect and fear,
and with sincerity of heart, just as you would obey Christ.

Ephesians 6:5

Lord, who may go and find refuge and shelter
in your tabernacle up on your holy hill?
Anyone who leads a blameless life and is truly sincere.

Psalm 15:1-2 TLB

May God's grace and blessing be upon all who
sincerely love our Lord Jesus Christ.

Ephesians 6:24 TLB

Let us come near to God with a sincere heart and a sure faith,
because we have been made free from a guilty conscience,
and our bodies have been washed with pure water.

Hebrews 10:22 NCV

THE END OF INSINCERITY

Some things are more adequately communicated by contrast. Take sincerity, for example.

King David experienced the heartrending and humiliating betrayal of his own son, though he had been faithful as a father. The kingdom for which he fought, prayed, and dedicated his whole existence was being stripped away by his offspring—Absalom. The handsome, charismatic son of the sovereign had convinced himself that he should occupy the throne, and thereby laid out a strategy to charm the king's subjects away with insincerity. He was marvelously successful until God exposed his greedy heart and set things right.

When well executed, gestures of insincerity are infectious and irresistible, appealing with flattery to the self-conceit of the one to whom they are directed. This sort of pretense is easy to disguise, and those who master it seem to have a propensity for even greater deceit, for the motives of insincerity are always suspect.

Most alarming is the discovery that insincerity can infect your own character. It is so convincing, even you can fall for your pretense. How can you protect yourself from practicing insincerity? That's a big question with a simple answer. Keep your feet firmly planted in the truth. Don't try to press your self-interests by being deceitful and insincere. Even if you are successful for a time, eventually your disingenuous ways will be exposed.

Absalom could have stood at his father's side in a seat of power and influence. He might even have become his heir, but instead he gambled everything on insincerity and lost.

Spiritual Growth

Make every effort to add to your faith goodness; and to goodness,
knowledge; and to knowledge, self-control; and to self-control,
perseverance; and to perseverance, godliness; and to godliness,
brotherly kindness; and to brotherly kindness, love.

2 Peter 1:5-7

As newborn babes, desire the pure milk of the word,
that you may grow thereby.

1 Peter 2:2 NKJV

Jesus said, "What is the seed that fell on the good ground?
That seed is like the person who hears the teaching and understands it.
That person grows and produces fruit."

Matthew 13:23 NCV

We must become like a mature person, growing until we become like
Christ and have his perfection. . . . Speaking the truth with love, we will
grow up in every way into Christ, who is the head.

Ephesians 4:13,15 NCV

We pray that you will also have great wisdom and understanding in
spiritual things so that you will live the kind of life that honors and
pleases the Lord in every way. You will produce fruit in every good work
and grow in the knowledge of God.

Colossians 1:9-10 NCV

THE TRUE MARK OF MATURITY

A certain diligence is required for growth in spiritual matters to occur. It doesn't happen by default. The apostle Peter describes it as the process in which you focus attention on issues of character. Trusting in the Lord, you discipline your heart to be good and to do good. Not just any goodness, but that which belongs to Christ—the goodness that reached from the Cross to embrace an undeserving world.

Goodness must be accompanied by knowledge—an experiential knowledge of the Son, and an understanding of the Father's will. Knowledge of the truth is the experience of grace.

Knowledge must be kept under the Spirit's control in order to be useful and effective. What you know in your head won't make up for what is lacking in your heart.

Self-control leads to the development of perseverance, because it is one of the most difficult of all disciplines. You persevere in the temptation to lose control, or worse yet, to take control.

Perseverance will produce godliness if your heart is fixed on the Lord. Godliness is the product that comes out of the kiln of character refinement.

Godliness should not be isolated in a monastery or sterilized in its application, for it is the very trait of God which nurtures brotherly affection. It must reach out to others for its very nature is to give.

Finally, brotherly kindness should affect unrivaled love. Love is, after all, the true mark of maturity.

Strength

Finally, be strong in the Lord and in his mighty power.
Put on the full armor of God so that you can take your stand against
the devil's schemes. For our struggle is not against flesh and blood,
but against . . . the powers of this dark world and . . .
the spiritual forces of evil.

Ephesians 6:10-12

I love you, LORD; you are my strength.

Psalm 18:1 NLT

I pray that from his glorious, unlimited resources he will give you
mighty inner strength through his Holy Spirit.

Ephesians 3:16 NLT

We are joined together in his body by his strong sinews, and we grow
only as we get our nourishment and strength from God.

Colossians 2:19 NLT

May our Lord Jesus Christ and God our Father, who loved us and in his
special favor gave us everlasting comfort and good hope, comfort your
hearts and give you strength in every good thing you do and say.

2 Thessalonians 2:16-17 NLT

SPIRITUAL RESOURCES

The strength you need for your life on earth is not derived from human resources; it comes straight from heaven's store. The problem with your mortal strength is that it imposes the same limitations on you as does your temporal existence: You have only enough power to manage what is already manageable. Strength for anything that exceeds your natural abilities must come from some source greater than yourself.

Since the struggle that you face in this life is not within the scope of your being—flesh and blood—then you must find resources comparable to the element in which your worst foe exists—the spiritual realm.

Jesus is the human link to divine strength. Because God took on the nature of man, He made it possible for man to access the nature of God. Thus you, being human, have spiritual resources available in Jesus, which are more powerful than any force your spiritual enemy can muster.

The armory that supplies you with this mighty power when you most need it consists of the disciplines of a Spirit-filled life: truth, righteousness, peace, faith, salvation, the Word, and prayer. Your diligence in practicing these disciplines determines the outcome of the battle.

Do you need strength? Get honest, get right with God, pursue peace with all men, be courageous in your faith, be confident in Him who saved you, be proficient in the Word, and pray as if your life depends upon it; for, in fact, it does.

Thankfulness

The LORD is my strength and my shield;
my heart trusts in him, and I am helped.
My heart leaps for joy
and I will give thanks to him in song.

Psalm 28:7

I will give you thanks in the great assembly;
among throngs of people I will praise you.

Psalm 35:18

It is good to give thanks to the LORD,
And to sing praises to Your name, O Most High;
To declare Your lovingkindness in the morning,
And Your faithfulness every night

Psalm 92:1-2 NKJV

In everything give thanks;
for this is the will of God in Christ Jesus for you.

1 Thessalonians 5:18 NKJV

By Him let us continually offer the sacrifice of praise to God,
that is, the fruit of our lips, giving thanks to His name.

Hebrews 13:15 NKJV

Heavenly Father,

How can I say thank You? Words alone could never suffice. You created me in Your own image, gave me the power to make my own choices, and bought me back when I sold myself to an unrighteous bidder. You have walked with me throughout the ups and downs of my earthly life, comforting, guiding, and teaching me. You have called me friend and made me worthy of sonship.

You are the One, Lord, who loves me unconditionally and forgives my almost constant transgressions. You are the One who has given me the gift of the Holy Spirit. And You, Lord, are the One who has gone on ahead to prepare an eternal dwelling for me when this life is past. Thank You for Your grace, Your provision, and Your faithfulness.

Amen.

I WANT TO THANK YOU!

One day, nine Jewish men along with one foreigner stood at a distance from Jesus and made loud solicitations for healing. They couldn't go near the newly acclaimed Rabbi because of their disease. The Lord answered, advising them to observe the procedures laid out in the Law of Moses by going first to the priest to confirm their leprosy. Likely they had failed to keep that ordinance when they contracted the dreaded illness, because confirmed leprosy meant banishment and exile. They reasoned that they might as well be dead, so why bother. However, Jesus never sanctioned neglect of the Law; He had come to fulfill it.

The lepers turned, in obedient response, to do what the Law demanded, heading for the nearest priest; their prompt obedience revealing their desperate faith and giving them access to the healing they sought.

Suddenly, one of the lepers, the foreigner, noticed a strange sensation.

"I feel a tingling in my fingertips," he said.

"What are you talking about? You don't have any nerve endings left," another chided.

"Look!" he stood gawking, holding his hands at eye level. "My skin is as smooth as a baby's behind!"

The others stood looking at themselves and each other, amazed.

"Jesus!" the foreigner turned shouting. "Thank You!" He broke into a run, sprinting across the terrain toward the Lord. "Wait, Lord! I want to thank You!"

Jesus turned, smiling. The man fell onto his face at Jesus' feet, crying and shouting praise to God. (See Luke 17:11-19).

My Precious Child,

Your praise and thanksgiving resounds in My ears like a lovely, enchanting melody; they rise to Me like an offering of sweet-smelling incense. I receive them as a precious treasure, found only after a long and difficult search.

Your heartfelt thanks causes Me to pour out even more favor upon you, filling to overflowing your cup of blessing. My arm of salvation is extended on your behalf, and My constant love will watch over you all your days. When you come before My throne, I will eagerly welcome you. I will give you eternal life and lead you in the ways of wisdom and understanding. I will be your God, time without end.

Your loving Father

Thoughts

I hope my words and thoughts please you.
LORD, you are my Rock, the one who saves me.

Psalm 19:14 NCV

Be careful what you think,
because your thoughts run your life.

Proverbs 4:23 NCV

Whoever loves pure thoughts and kind words
will have even the king as a friend.

Proverbs 22:11 NCV

Let heaven fill your thoughts.
Do not think only about things down here on earth.

Colossians 3:2 NLT

Whatever is true, whatever is noble, whatever is right, whatever is pure,
whatever is lovely, whatever is admirable—if anything is excellent or
praiseworthy—think about such things.

Philippians 4:8

PLACES YOU NEVER INTENDED TO GO

Some people like to say, "My thoughts are my own." But are they—really? It seems that your thoughts may have a will of their own. Unless you round them up and tame them, bringing them into obedience to God, they could take you places you never intended to go. Consider what the Bible says:

Angry thoughts . . . "Anyone who is angry with his brother will be subject to judgment" (Matthew 5:22).

Impure thoughts . . . "Anyone who looks at a woman lustfully has already committed adultery with her in his heart" (Matthew 5:28).

Worrisome thoughts . . . "Do not worry about your life. . . . But seek first His kingdom and his righteousness, and all these things will be given to you as well" (Matthew 6:25, 33).

Judgmental thoughts . . . "Do not judge, or you too will be judged. For in the same way you judge others, you will be judged, and with the measure you use, it will be measured to you" (Matthew 7:1).

Forgiving thoughts . . . "If you forgive men when they sin against you, your heavenly Father will also forgive you. But if you do not forgive men their sins, your Father will not forgive your sins" (Matthew 6:14-15).

Loving thoughts . . . "Love is patient, love is kind. It does not envy, it does not boast, it is not proud. It is not rude, it is not self-seeking, it is not easily angered, it keeps no record of wrongs. . . . It always protects, always trusts, always hopes, always perseveres" (1 Corinthians 13:4-7).

When your thoughts are wayward, offer them to God and let Him bring them into line. And when your thoughts are good, offer them to God as an act of worship.

Time

It is time to seek the LORD,
that he may come and rain righteousness upon you.

Hosea 10:12 NRSV

LORD, remind me how brief my time on earth will be.
Remind me that my days are numbered,
and that my life is fleeing away.

Psalm 39:4 NLT

O my people, trust in him at all times.
Pour out your heart to him,
for God is our refuge.

Psalm 62:8 NLT

See then that you walk circumspectly, not as fools but as wise,
redeeming the time, because the days are evil.

Ephesians 5:15-16 NKJV

To every thing there is a season,
and a time to every purpose under the heaven.

Ecclesiastes 3:1 KJV

Heavenly Father,

It's seems like I'm always running, always busy, always distracted. Sure, I pray. I even feel that tugging inside to pour out my heart to You—but something always gets in the way. Usually, it's something trifling, something mundane, but still I let it capture me and steal the moments that should have belonged to You.

Help me, Lord, to find time to be with You. Wake me in the morning. Keep me awake in the evening. Open a space during the day. I want more of You. I need to be filled with Your strength and wisdom. I know it's my time and my responsibility. It's just that I've tried so many times and failed. Add Your perfect touch to my imperfect will that together we can make my time count for Your eternal purposes.

Amen.

AWAY FROM THE CROWDS

After burying his body, the disciples of John the Baptist run to Jesus for refuge. The Lord's great heart staggers under the crushing weight of their news, and He gets into a boat to get away from the masses of people. He needs time alone . . . time for reflection, time for prayer, and time to consider His own mission in light of John's brutal murder.

Relentless in their demands, the crowd follows—a multitude of disheartened, bewildered people. Seeing their confusion and fear, His heart moves with compassion while His hands move to break bread. Jesus feeds them, consoles them, and sends them away satisfied.

Maybe now He can get away to pray. He sends the disciples across the water, assuring them that He will soon follow on foot.

Exhausted, but finally alone, Jesus passes the night in prayer. His precious friend John—known to the crowds as the Baptist—has finished his mission. How long before Jesus must follow? Occasionally, He gazes across the water to see how His friends are faring, for a strong wind stirs, offering enough resistance to keep their small fishing vessel from shore. He rises from his rocky altar—it is time.

In the wee hours of the morning, Jesus comes walking on the water looking to the disciples like some ghost fresh out of the tomb. He climbs into the boat, calming their fears and hushing the wind, and in an instant, they reach the other shore. It is time to move on with His mission, for time is running out. (See Mark 6:29-56).

We are all given time enough to invest in eternal life. Don't let time run out on you.

My Precious Child,

I understand that your life is full of obligations and responsibilities. I know you must feel like there are never enough hours in the day. I'm not asking for all of your time—just enough each day to ensure the connection between us, enough to refill your cup with love, joy, peace, and power.

You are precious to me. I created you for a purpose, and I want to see you fulfill that purpose in the time you've been given here on earth. Come to Me—in the wee hours of the morning or the dark hours of the night. Speak to Me when the sun is full in the sky or when it is brilliantly stretched across the horizon. I am always here waiting, hoping that you will make time for Me.

Your loving Father

Trials

By wise counsel you will wage your own war,
And in a multitude of counselors there is safety.

Proverbs 24:6 NKJV

Let us fix our eyes on Jesus, the author and perfecter of our faith,
who for the joy set before him endured the cross, scorning its shame,
and sat down at the right hand of the throne of God. Consider him who
endured such opposition from sinful men, so that you
will not grow weary and lose heart.

Hebrews 12:2-3

Be truly glad! There is wonderful joy ahead, even though it is necessary
for you to endure many trials for a while. These trials are only to test
your faith, to show that it is strong and pure. It is being tested as fire tests
and purifies gold. . . . So if your faith remains strong after being tried by
fiery trials, it will bring you much praise and glory and honor on the day
when Jesus Christ is revealed to the whole world.

1 Peter 1:6-7 NLT

We can rejoice . . . when we run into problems and trials, for we know
that they are good for us—they help us learn to endure.

Romans 5:3 NLT

TIPS FOR FACING TRIBULATION

In the year 445 B.C., during the reign of Artaxerxes in Persia, an Israelite named Nehemiah served as the king's cupbearer. Upon learning that the walls of Jerusalem were in ruin, he set out to restore the holy city with the king's blessing. But Nehemiah quickly encountered severe trials. A strong opponent of Israel threatened Nehemiah and his helpers in an attempt to stop the restoration.

The strategy Nehemiah employed proved very effective. Consider his techniques when facing trials of your own.

1) He made a thorough evaluation of the situation while his opposition was asleep. It is critical to be objective in assessing your circumstances without the scrutiny and pressure of the opposition.

2) He devised a plan. As the saying goes, "If you fail to plan, you plan to fail."

3) He enlisted the help of dependable people. It is wise to solicit the help and support of trustworthy confidants.

4) He met the threats of his opponents with humility and courage. Nehemiah confronted every new struggle with prayer and determination.

5) He remained diligent, refusing to allow the trial to halt his progress.

6) He remained faithful. He kept his focus on God's purpose.

7) He posted a guard where there were vulnerabilities. Nehemiah knew where his weaknesses were, and he carefully watched over them.

8) He refused to be distracted. Ignoring the badgering insults of his opponent, he kept his mind on his work.

9) He followed through to the finish. Nehemiah finished the work in fifty-two days! The completion of his task put an end to his trial, as well.

Trust

Those who know the LORD trust him,
because he will not leave those who come to him.

Psalm 9:10 NCV

My enemy will say, "I have overcome him,"
and my foes will rejoice when I fall.
But I trust in your unfailing love;
my heart rejoices in your salvation.

Psalm 13:4-5

The king trusts in the LORD;
through the unfailing love of the Most High
he will not be shaken.

Psalm 21:7

The LORD is my strength and my shield;
my heart trusts in him, and I am helped.
My heart leaps for joy
and I will give thanks to him in song.

Psalm 28:7

THE LIONS' DEN

In the year 541 B.C., a man named Daniel whispers from on his knees, "Lord, King Darius has issued a decree that no man should pray to any but to him alone." The faithful old Hebrew pauses to stare out the window toward Jerusalem. "Please don't hold it against him, for he was led astray by the flattery of deceitful men seeking power."

A commotion interrupts Daniel's prayer as three men burst into his dwelling. Pointing an accusing finger, one shouts, "A lawbreaker!" Taking Daniel by force, they lead him to Darius's throne room.

"O King, live forever!" one of the men begins. "This man was found praying to the God of Israel in spite of your command that no one should pray to any god but you, O King."

The king is suddenly animated with anger. "You fools, this is Daniel—a man of great integrity and tremendous ability. His God has blessed him because of his worthy life. You've schemed against this honest man to keep him from a position of influence."

"Nevertheless," the antagonist replies, "your decree cannot be revoked. This insurgent must be punished by death."

"Bait the lions!" another of the men calls to the some servants standing nearby.

"May the God in whom you trust rescue you, Daniel," Darius laments just as Daniel is shoved into the pit.

At the break of dawn, after a sleepless night, Darius rushes to the mouth of the den. "Daniel!" he calls in anguish.

"O King, live forever!" Daniel echoes. (See Daniel 6).

If God can be trusted to close the mouths of hungry lions, how much more can He be trusted to hear and answer your prayers?

Truth

The Lord's promise is sure. He speaks no careless word;
all he says is purest truth, like silver seven times refined.

Psalm 12:6 TLB

Cross-examine me, O Lord, and see that this is so;
test my motives and affections too. For I have taken
your loving-kindness and your truth as my ideals.

Psalm 26:2-3 TLB

A wise person is hungry for truth, while the fool feeds on trash.

Proverbs 15:14 NLT

We will not hide these truths from our children
but will tell the next generation about the glorious deeds of the LORD.
We will tell of his power and the mighty miracles he did.

Psalm 78:4 NLT

Truth stands the test of time; lies are soon exposed.

Proverbs 12:19 NLT

Our responsibility is never to oppose the truth,
but to stand for the truth at all times.

2 Corinthians 13:8 NLT

Heavenly Father,

I feel like I've spent my whole life in a search for truth. It has been a long and disappointing journey. But finally, I have made my way back to where I began—back to You.

Thank You for being patient, Lord, while I checked out many systems of thought that claimed to be the truth. All of them were illusions based on misguided, though sometimes well-intended, philosophies that eventually ended in self-indulgence and emptiness. I'm grieved to think about the time I wasted—while You waited.

All I want now is to be grounded in You, my living Lord, for You are the embodiment of truth, having faced death and overcome it. No other contender can make that claim. None but You.

Amen.

✸

I TELL YOU THE TRUTH

"I tell you the truth . . ."

Jesus coined this familiar phrase at the inauguration of His ministry and spoke it all the way through to the Cross.

Early in His ministry, Jesus visits Nazareth, His hometown, and attends the synagogue, as is His habit. This occasion serves as the springboard for His teaching and healing ministry.

News about Him has spread, and His kinsfolk are happy to have their hometown celebrity back. That is, until He lets them down. They want Him to do a miracle for them as He did in Capernaum. After all, doesn't He owe them that, being neighbors and all?

The kingdom of God is not about sensationalism; it's about salvation. It isn't about religiosity; it's about relationship. It isn't a bunch of hype; it's about humility and service. Jesus worked miracles not to satisfy morbid curiosity but to demonstrate and confirm spiritual truths in the interest of rescuing the hearts of men and women.

"I tell you the truth," He says. "No prophet is accepted in his hometown" (Luke 4:24).

Indignant, they try to push Him over a cliff. (See Luke 4:14-30).

Now to the Cross. One of the thieves hanging beside Jesus is converted. His heart is touched by Jesus' tender mercy when He said, "Father, forgive them, for they do not know what they are doing" (Luke 23:34).

"I tell you the truth," Jesus said to him. "Today you will be with Me in paradise" (Luke 23:43).

Truth is spoken, on the one hand, to those who turn away from Him in disbelief, and on the other hand, to those who turn to Him in faith.

What have you done with the truth He has spoken to you?

My Precious Child,

All the philosophies of the world contain some element of truth. Some advocate love for all; others, service. Some encourage sacrifice; others, self-worth. But they are, in the end, only thinly veiled substitutes for *the* Truth. These philosophies are not new; they've been around in one form or another since the beginning. It seems that men and women will never stop believing that somehow they can make atonement for their own sins. But that can be done only through a sinless sacrifice.

The truth is, My child, that all their striving is futile—and unnecessary. I've already provided a perfect substitute—My precious Son, Jesus Christ. That's why He said of Himself, "I am the way and the truth and the life. No one comes to the Father except through me" (John 14:6). Welcome home, My child.

Your loving Father

Understanding

We have not stopped . . . asking God to fill you with the knowledge
of his will through all spiritual wisdom and understanding.
And we pray this in order that you may live a life worthy of the Lord
and may please him in every way.

Colossians 1:9-10

My mouth shall speak wisdom;
the meditation of my heart shall be understanding.

Psalm 49:3 RSV

The fear of the LORD is the beginning of wisdom;
a good understanding have all those who practice it.
His praise endures for ever!

Psalm 111:10 RSV

I have more understanding than the elders,
for I obey your precepts.
I gain understanding from your precepts;
therefore I hate every wrong path.

Psalm 119:100,104

I pray also that you will have greater understanding in your heart so you
will know the hope to which he has called us and that you will know how
rich and glorious are the blessings God has promised his holy people.

Ephesians 1:18 NCV

THE SPIRIT GIVES

Concerning Jesus, Isaiah the prophet wrote: "The Spirit of the LORD will rest on him—the Spirit of wisdom and of understanding, the Spirit of counsel and of power, the Spirit of knowledge and of the fear of the LORD" (Isaiah 11:2).

The Spirit gave Jesus wisdom and understanding; and Jesus understood, all right. He understood that the God of His people was His real Father. He comprehended what the will of the Father was. He grasped what was His role in the Father's will—His mission among men. Jesus realized the need men had for salvation—the lost condition of their souls. He knew their desperate need for forgiveness and pardon. Jesus took to heart the responsibility to teach truth and give grace, where each applied. He was able to discern the tiniest trace of faith in the hearts of men, and to mine out the cynicism that opposed the work of the Almighty. Yes, Jesus had understanding, and He used it to accomplish His mission here on earth.

The amazing thing is that the apostle Paul wrote that all believers everywhere could have that same understanding – given by the same Spirit.

The agent of understanding in Jesus' life and ministry is the very same as yours—the Spirit. Imagine how powerful and effective your life could be if you had a heart of understanding comparable to His. You would be able to pursue the purpose for which you were created and make full use of the gifts and callings God has placed on your life. Imagine that—and then seek Him for it. He promises to give it freely, but only to those who seek it.

Unity

Make every effort to keep the unity of the Spirit
through the bond of peace.

Ephesians 4:3

How very good and pleasant it is
when kindred live together in unity!

Psalm 133:1 NRSV

Jesus looked up to heaven and said, "Father . . . I have given
them the glory you gave me—the glorious unity of being one, as we are—
I in them and you in me, all being perfected into one—so that the world
will know you sent me and will understand that you love them
as much as you love me."

John 17:1,22-23 TLB

It was he who gave some to be apostles, some to be prophets,
some to be evangelists, and some to be pastors and teachers,
to prepare God's people for works of service, so that the body of Christ
may be built up until we all reach unity in the faith and in the knowledge
of the Son of God and become mature, attaining to the whole measure
of the fullness of Christ. From him the whole body, joined and held
together by every supporting ligament, grows and builds itself up
in love, as each part does its work.

Ephesians 4:11-13,16

A COMMON END

The cells in your body have an amazing capacity for communicating with each other as a strategy for growth and survival. This method of communication is so effective it keeps every system—cardiovascular, pulmonary, digestive, nervous, muscular—in sync and running like a machine. Or more like a technological wonder. The key to the body's miraculous rhythm is that every cell executes its task in harmony with the rest. Your brain is workshop central for your body's functional processes and sends signals that cause each system to do its job on cue. The whole comprises the unity essential for your existence.

Unity is not uniformity. Uniformity means to conform to one standard, rule, or form. If all cells were alike, your body wouldn't be a body at all, just one big blob of identical cells. Unity, on the other hand, carries no suggestion of conformity. It implies harmony— different variables working together toward a common end.

The body, and its functioning, is a metaphor used in Scripture in reference to the community of believers. God's people are a diversified lot comprised of many shapes, sizes, thoughts, opinions, personalities, and perspectives. With all of those differences, all Christians everywhere still acknowledge and serve the same Lord.

According to the apostle Paul, Christians are to be diligent to keep the unity of the Spirit. Just as every cell has its individual function and responsibility in maintaining your life, every individual has that responsibility in the Spirit. And just like the cells in the body, your ability to keep the unity is contingent on your connection with the head, which is Christ.

Fix your eyes, your mind, and your heart upon Him.

Unselfishness

Let all men know and perceive and recognize your unselfishness
(your considerateness, your forbearing spirit).

Philippians 4:5 AMP

Do nothing from selfishness or conceit, but in humility count others
better than yourselves. Let each of you look not only to his own interests,
but also to the interests of others.

Philippians 2:3-4 RSV

Where jealousy and selfish ambition exist, there will be disorder
and every vile practice. But the wisdom from above is first pure,
then peaceable, gentle, open to reason, full of mercy and good fruits.

James 3:16-17 RSV

Those who belong to Christ Jesus have crucified their own sinful selves.
They have given up their old selfish feelings and the evil things
they wanted to do.

Galatians 5:24 NCV

Jesus said to the disciples, "If any of you wants to be my follower,
you must put aside your selfish ambition, shoulder your cross,
and follow me."

Matthew 16:24 NLT

Heavenly Father,

I have to confess that I've lived my life almost completely to suit my own selfish desires and ambitions. I've pressed my agenda at the expense of others and given little thought to any interests other than my own. I've withheld my love and affection from those who have refused to do things my way and put myself first in almost every situation. As a result, my life is in ruins, my heart is empty, and all my lofty achievements are as vapor.

I've made poor choices, Lord. I've done things my way. I only pray that it's not too late to start doing things Your way. Have mercy on me and rid me of my selfish ways. Help me to rebuild my life on a foundation of selfless love.

Amen.

GRANDFATHER'S WATCH

One day Jim received a gift from his father-in-law. It was an antique, gold pocket watch that had belonged to his wife's grandfather Buck prior to his death. Representing his surname, the initial B was engraved on the front cover of the watch. "Big Buck," as the family called him, had managed quite a legacy, leaving all of the young men of the family to esteem him as a hero.

Jim was thrilled with the heirloom and promptly purchased a fob with which to attach it to his vest. Thus he proudly carried the watch for many days thereafter.

One day, while conversing with two of his wife's nephews, Jim unwittingly discovered that his father-in-law—grandfather to the boys—had given the older of them a watch belonging to Big Buck, as well. Unfortunately, Luke, the younger grandson, had been overlooked many times and in many ways because of his grandfather's bias toward his older cousin. It had gone a long way to deteriorate his self-confidence and sense of worth.

Jim saw the wound in Luke's eyes when he learned of the gift of the watch. Waiting for a private moment, Jim approached him while gently releasing the fob from his vest. He held it out in his palm, saying, "Luke, I want you to have this watch. It belonged to your great-grandfather."

"But, Uncle Jim," Luke stammered, "that's your watch now, and it's worth a lot of money."

"Take it, Son," Jim urged. "See, to me it's just a great watch. But to you it's a part of your heritage, and it belonged to a man you admired."

An unselfish heart can be used by God to mend a broken heart.

My Precious Child,

I've been waiting for you to come face to face with the vanity and selfishness in your life. It has carried you far from Me—but not so far away that I can't reach and touch your repentant heart, reclaiming you for My own. It was hard for Me to let you go your own way, knowing that your path would take you to emptiness and heartache. But your choices are your own. I knew that the day would come when your selfish heart would run its course, realize its errant ways, and turn again to Me.

Today is the first day of a new life for you. It's a day of forgiveness and renewal and victory over sin. Take My hand, and we'll walk together along the path of selfless love and abundant blessing.

Your loving Father

Victory

Do not be afraid as you go out to fight today! Do not lose heart or panic. For the LORD your God is going with you! He will fight for you against your enemies, and he will give you victory!

Deuteronomy 20:3-4 NLT

In all these things we have full victory through God who showed his love for us.

Romans 8:37 NCV

Death's power to hurt is sin, and the power of sin is the law. But we thank God! He gives us the victory through our Lord Jesus Christ.

1 Corinthians 15:56-57 NCV

The LORD is my strength and my song;
he has become my victory.
Songs of joy and victory are sung in the camp of the godly.
The strong right arm of the LORD has done glorious things!

Psalm 118:14-15 NLT

Everyone who is a child of God conquers the world.
And this is the victory that conquers the world—our faith.

1 John 5:4 NCV

I HAVE OVERCOME

Just before His death, Jesus spoke with His closest friends about what they would face without Him. They had grown accustomed to His presence and His power, and He knew that His crucifixion—the very purpose for which He came—would seem to them like a total defeat, even though, in fact, it heralded their greatest victory.

Jesus offered three practical pieces of advice that reach through the expanse of time and space to effectively bring victory to any situation in any culture.

First, Jesus said to realize that "in this world you will have trouble" (John 16:33). The sooner we accept that life is a series of difficulties, the better equipped we will be to overcome.

However, Jesus also said, "Do not let your hearts be troubled" (John 14:27). Worry is not only a waste of emotional energy; it inhibits the rational abilities of intelligent people. Attack anxiety with clear-headed thinking. Enlist the help of a friend or family member, if necessary, to ensure that you are being objective and reasonable.

Finally, Jesus completed His counsel by saying, "and do not be afraid" (John 14:27). Fear is the offspring of anxiety. If you indulge yourself in worry, you'll convince yourself to be afraid. The greatest percentage of our fears never become reality, yet we expend important resources dealing with them. Confidence and courage come from trusting in God to equip and empower us with the ability to effectively deal with our difficulties.

In light of these three practical admonitions, Jesus concluded by saying, "Take heart! I have overcome the world" (John 16:33). Neither this life, nor its troubles, will endure forever. The ultimate victory—Jesus' resurrection from the grave—will one day be ours as well.

Wisdom

These are the proverbs of King Solomon of Israel, David's son:
He wrote them to teach his people how to live—how to act
in every circumstance, for he wanted them to be understanding,
just and fair in everything they did.

Proverbs 1:1-3 TLB

Fools think their own way is right,
but the wise listen to advice.

Proverbs 12:15 NRSV

How can men be wise? The only way to begin is by reverence for God.
For growth in wisdom comes from obeying his laws.
Praise his name forever.

Psalm 111:10 TLB

Who is wise and understanding among you? . . . If you harbor bitter
envy and selfish ambition in your hearts, do not boast about it or
deny the truth. Such "wisdom" does not come down from heaven
but is earthly, unspiritual, of the devil. For where you have envy
and selfish ambition, there you find disorder and every evil practice.
But the wisdom that comes from heaven is first of all pure; then
peace-loving, considerate, submissive, full of mercy and good fruit,
impartial and sincere.

James 3:13-17

Heavenly Father,

It turns out that life is much more complicated than I thought, and I need some help sorting it all out. It's not the black-and-white, right-and-wrong issues that concern me. Even though I don't always want to do the right thing, it isn't difficult to know what I should do. It's those gray areas that bother me, when things aren't so clearly defined.

For those choices, Lord, I need wisdom—the insight that brings order and clarity to the situation. I need to be able to look at the facts and see them from a different perspective—Your perspective. Only then can I be sure that I'm living my life to the fullest, making the most of the possibilities You've placed before me, and honoring my responsibilities.

Amen.

A HEART OF WISDOM

When it comes to relationships, wisdom is one of your most pressing needs. Yet not just any wisdom will suffice. There are two distinct varieties: spiritual and unspiritual (James 3:13-18).

How can you know the difference? Unspiritual wisdom is the wisdom that wants to get ahead at any cost. Spiritual wisdom, on the other hand, is a matter of discernment and understanding (James 3:17). It has others' interests at heart.

- Are you pure in heart and motive in your relationships?
- Do you strive for peace with the Lord, with yourself, and with the community?
- Do you show respect and consideration, preserving others' dignity no matter what happens?
- Are you merciful, compassionate, and tenderhearted toward others?
- Do your actions reflect the fruit of the Spirit: love, joy, peace, patience, kindness, goodness, faithfulness, gentleness, and self-control?
- Is your judgment and treatment of others impartial and unbiased?
- Are you sincerely loving, genuinely interested, authentically invested, and truly seeking the best for others?

Examine your heart . . . for wisdom . . . selfish or unselfish.

My Precious Child,

I've seen you struggling to do the right thing—and that shows that you are already becoming a wise person, because wisdom will always pursue righteousness and truth. Your heart is in the right place, but you may not be using all your resources.

The next time you encounter one of those gray areas, stop right where you are and pray. It doesn't have to be a long prayer filled with fancy words—just a simple "Lord, help me" will do. You see, I've promised to give wisdom to anyone who asks for it—unconditionally. You ask—I give. The formula is that simple. I'll change up the situation a little so you can see it from a different angle. And I won't ever think you are silly or childish for asking. You have My word on that.

Your loving Father

Work

Do your work with enthusiasm. Work as if you were serving the Lord, not as if you were serving only men and women.

Ephesians 6:7 NCV

My life is worth nothing unless I use it for doing the work assigned me by the Lord Jesus.

Acts 20:24 NLT

In all the work you are doing, work the best you can. Work as if you were doing it for the Lord, not for people. Remember that you will receive your reward from the Lord, which he promised to his people. You are serving the Lord Christ.

Colossians 3:23-24 NCV

To enjoy your work and to accept your lot in life—that is indeed a gift from God. The person who does that will not need to look back with sorrow on his past, for God gives him joy.

Ecclesiastes 5:19-20 TLB

When you eat the labor of your hands, You shall be happy, and it shall be well with you.

Psalm 128:2 NKJV

PRESS FORWARD

Brad was a good, solid hitter. With a batting average of .450, he always got on base but rarely got further than first base.

"Son, if you would stop looking at the ball once you've made contact, you would be scoring twice as much as you are now," Coach Miller kept telling him.

"I try to remember, Coach. I really do." Brad knocked a dirt clod off of his cleats with a bat. "It's like I'm running from the ball or something."

"That's it!" the coach grabbed Brad by the shoulders. "The trouble is your perspective. You think that you are running *from* the ball, Brad. But the point is, you are running *to* the base. You need to fix your eyes on the goal, not the ball, and run with all of your might. Never, never look back."

Going forward is hard work for anybody. The temptation to look over your shoulder is almost irresistible. You intend to make steady progress into the future—toward your goal—but you cannot resist the urge to look back. And you end up running from things that haunt you, frighten you, tempt you, or make you feel guilty. Those things are a downward drag on your spiritual sprint. They cumber you with a heavy heart and clutter your thinking so that you can't be free and creative.

The task at hand is to press forward, working hard to forget the prison of your past. The work Jesus did at Calvary was sufficient to handle it!

We do not need to go "somewhere" to find God,

any more than the fish need to soar to find the ocean

or the eagle needs to plunge to find the air.

RUFUS MATTHEW JONES

TOPICAL INDEX